D1727751

AN INTRODUCTION
TO THE ANGLO-AMERICAN LEGAL SYSTEM

The Global Law Collection
Textbook Series
Director: Rafael Domingo

TONI M. FINE

Assistant Dean, Fordham University School of Law, New York

AN INTRODUCTION TO THE ANGLO-AMERICAN LEGAL SYSTEM

THOMSON

TM

ARANZADI

Primera edición, 2007

Reimpresión, agosto 2011

© Toni M. Fine - 2007
© Editorial Aranzadi, SA

Editorial Aranzadi, SA
Camino de Galar, 15
31190 Cizur Menor (Navarra)

Imprime: Rodona Industria Gráfica, SL
          Polígono Agustinos, Calle A, Nave D-11
          31013 - Pamplona

Depósito Legal: NA 1044/2007

ISBN: 978-84-8355-088-5

El editor no se hace responsable de las opiniones recogidas, comentarios y manifestaciones vertidas por los autores. La presente obra recoge exclusivamente la opinión de su autor como manifestación de su derecho de libertad de expresión.

Reservados todos los derechos en España. El contenido de esta publicación no puede ser reproducido, ni en todo ni en parte, ni transmitido, ni registrado por ningún sistema de recuperación de información, en ninguna forma ni por ningún medio, sin el permiso previo, por escrito, de Editorial Aranzadi, SA.

Index

Chapter III

CHAPTER I

OPENING THOUGHTS – DEFINING ELEMENTS OF THE U.S. COMMON LAW SYSTEM

Although it would be difficult to characterize the Anglo-American legal system[1] in a few pages, it is possible for purposes of this brief introduction to identify certain defining aspects: *First*, U.S. governmental structures are marked by notable divisions of power, both vertical and horizontal. *Second*, there are various sources of law in the U.S. legal system. Sources of law derive from each branch of the government at both the state and the federal levels, and from an impressive array of secondary authorities that range from those that are highly influential to those that are far less so. *Third*, the U.S. legal system is distinguished by the primacy of one of these sources of law – case law. Under certain circumstances, case law is obligatory under principles of *stare decisis*, a policy under which judicial holdings are followed in subsequent cases involving the same legal issue and similar material facts. *Finally*, the litigation system in the United States claims many unique attributes. Each of these aspects is discussed briefly below and in more depth in the chapters that follow.

First: The nature of governmental structures (Chapter II) – Governmental structures in the United States are characterized by notable divisions of power. The framers of the Constitution of the United States sought to diffuse power as much as possible in order to prevent the accumulation of too much power in any one person or body. Such a division of governmental power, it was thought, would best preserve the rights and liberties of individuals. *Federalism* is an important constitutional arrangement under which powers are divided between a national (or federal) government on the one hand, and the several state governments on the other hand. In the United States, the federal government is a government of broad authority, but it is a government of limited powers – specifically, its authority is limited to the powers enumerated in the Constitution. The States retain considerable powers. Within each sovereign, *i.e.*, the national government and each state, powers are further divided among the three branches of government – the legislative branch (responsible for law making), the executive branch (responsible for carrying out, or executing, the law), and the judicial branch (responsible for interpreting the law). This separation of powers is supplemented by a system of checks and balances whereby

---

1. The term «Anglo-American» is used to represent the legal system of the United States of America, which has its roots in English common law.

each branch retains some controls or «checks» over each of the other branches. Constitutionally mandated by the U.S. Constitution with respect to the national government, each of the states has a constitution that provides for a similar system of separated but shared or overlapping powers. Moreover, there are certain rights that are retained by the people and that are not subject to government interference, or that may be subject to government interference only upon a suitable showing of governmental need.

Second: U.S. judicial systems (Chapter III) – The United States is composed of a number of independent court systems – the federal court system, which is organized both hierarchically and geographically; and state court systems, which are controlled autonomously by each sovereign state. The Supreme Court of the United States is the ultimate arbiter of federal law, but the court of last resort of each state court system has the final say as to the interpretation of that state's laws. The dual nature of U.S. court systems gives rise to a number of complexities. For instance, federal courts are often called upon to interpret and apply state laws, and state courts are often required to interpret and apply federal law or the law of another state.

Third: Sources of law (Chapter IV) – Anglo-American law is the product of many different sources of law, which can be divided into *primary* and *secondary* sources of law. Because of the duality of government systems under the U.S. system of federalism, primary sources of law are created at both the federal and the state levels. These sources of law are worthy of differing levels of respect based on principles of supremacy (under which valid federal law supersedes conflicting state law) and hierarchy (under which constitutional provisions take precedence over legislation, which takes precedence over executive issuances, which take precedence over case law). When there is no controlling primary authority, courts may consult non-binding primary authorities or a range of secondary sources of law.

Fourth: The primacy of case law (Chapter V) – Case law holds a position of special importance in the U.S. common law system. Reading, analyzing, and synthesizing case law is an integral aspect of law practice (and law study) in the United States. Under rules of *stare decisis*, precedent – earlier decided cases – may be binding on a subsequent court considering the same legal issue. In addition, although constitutional and statutory sources are superior to cases in the hierarchy of sources of law, relevant case law is consulted when interpreting or applying that (or a similar) provision in the future. In other words, courts in the U.S. do not undertake *de novo* interpretation of constitutional and statutory provisions in each case. Instead, they consult the decisional law that already exists as to the relevant provision, which precedent may or may not be binding.

Fifth: The adversarial system and its attributes (Chapter VI) – Under the U.S. adversarial system, the parties (through their attorneys) are responsible for the development of the entire case – facts and legal issues. The judge has a relatively passive role in many aspects of trial work, but is responsible for ensuring that evidentiary and other legal rules are followed and that the legal issues are properly presented to the jury. The jury, which consists of a group of laypersons convened for a specific trial, is charged with deciding the facts in dispute and with applying the law to those facts as instructed by the judge.

The U.S. litigation system is marked by several other distinctive characteristics. The presence of the jury as the finder of fact raises special challenges and presents unique dynamics. Procedures for pre-trial fact discovery in the United States are far more extensive than anywhere else in the world. Such procedures have been criticized as being an injurious feature of the system but they also have been touted as promoting rational settlements and for making trials proceed more smoothly and without strategic advantage based on surprise. In addition, large punitive damages may be awarded in the United States. Although such awards are not common, the possibility that they may be awarded does impact litigation and settlement strategies. These and a myriad of other peculiar characteristics of the U.S. legal system raise special challenges for students, practitioners, and judges.

CHAPTER II

THE CONSTITUTION OF THE UNITED STATES

I. INTRODUCTION

The Constitution of the United States is the national charter.[1] As such, the Constitution establishes and organizes the government and governmental institutions and defines (although in broad terms) the rights and liberties of its citizens. The Constitution is a carefully balanced document that provides for divisions of power and overlapping systems of authority. In doing so, it provides for a national government that is sufficiently strong to meet the needs of the nation, yet one that is limited in order to protect and preserve the rights of individuals and of the states as independent sovereigns. The sharing of governmental powers between the national government and the various state governments is the doctrine of federalism. The three distinct branches of the national government are assigned different duties («separation of powers»), but each has the obligation to cooperate with and monitor the other branches («checks and balances»). As James Madison wrote:

> In the compound republic of America, the power surrendered by the people is first divided between two distinct governments, and then the portion allocated to each subdivided among distinct and separate departments. Hence a double security arises to the rights of the people. The different governments will control each other, and at the same time each will be controlled by itself.[2]

The Constitution is a remarkably enduring document. In existence since 1787, it contains only twenty-seven amendments and its essential features have remained intact since its inception.

The U.S. Constitution is also a concise document. Consistent with the common law system in which it operates, the Constitution contains many broadly written provisions, leaving to the courts the task of developing the precise meaning of its terms through case law. This feature of the Constitution gives it the flexibility to adapt and evolve over time.

---

1. The Constitution of the United States is set forth as Appendix I.
2. Federalist No. 51, at 349 (James Madison) (Carl Van Doren, ed., The Easton Press 1979). The Federalist papers were a series of newspaper advertisements designed to promote and garner support for the proposed Constitution. They were written by Alexander Hamilton, James Madison, and John Jay, under the pseudonym «Plubius.»

II. A STRUCTURAL OVERVIEW OF THE CONSTITUTION OF THE UNITED STATES

The Constitution of the United States consists of three separate parts: The Preamble; the Articles, which comprise the body of the Constitution; and the Amendments.

A. THE PREAMBLE

The opening words of the Preamble to the Constitution of the United States – *We the People...* — are well known to most Americans and to many around the world. Although it is not an important textual source, the Preamble does evoke some of the primary themes contained in the body of the Constitution. The opening phrase itself suggests a delegation of power by a people of free will. The Preamble also reflects the notion that the *states* and the *people* themselves retain significant powers, and that the national government created by the Constitution is to be one of limited authority. These themes are expounded in other provisions of the Constitution, as will be discussed below, and represent the central character of the Constitution and the relationship between the federal government on the one hand and the states and the people on the other hand.

B. THE ARTICLES: THE BODY OF THE CONSTITUTION

The body of the Constitution is comprised of seven articles. These articles establish the structure of the government of the United States of America. In doing so, the Constitution creates a federal government in which powers are shared among the three branches – the legislature, the executive, and the judiciary. Importantly, the federal government established by the Constitution is a government of broad but limited, or enumerated, powers. Under the system of federalism that was created by the Constitution, the states retain exclusive authority over many important matters. The national government was delegated powers only to the extent that such authority was necessary to protect the national interest and security.[3]

C. THE AMENDMENTS

In its more than 200-year history, the Constitution has been amended only twenty-seven times. There are a number of reasons to explain this limited amendment history. First, the amendment process itself is extremely onerous and difficult to achieve. Second, the American public treats the Constitution with great respect and there is often reluctance toward approving formal amendments. Finally, the Constitution, as an evolving, «living» document, is in a sense continually modified as it is interpreted and applied by the courts,

---

3. See Part III, *infra*.

making formal amendments less important to the continuing viability of the U.S. Constitution.

III.   THE ARTICLES: GOVERNMENTAL STRUCTURES AND SHA-RED POWERS

The seven articles that make up the body of the U.S. Constitution establish the general structure and powers of the national (or federal) government, and define the relationship between the national government and the states. Section A. discusses the structure of the national government and the relationship between the three branches that comprise the federal government. Section B. discusses federalism – the relationship between the sovereign state governments and the national government.

The body of the Constitution also establishes a process by which the Constitution can be amended (Article V), protects the privileges and immunities of citizens (Article IV), and affords full faith and credit to public records, acts, and proceedings in one state by the other states (Article VI). The final article provides for the ratification of the Constitution (Article VII).

A.   THE NATIONAL GOVERNMENT: SEPARATION OF POWERS AND CHECKS AND BALANCES

The Constitution establishes a balanced national government by separating powers among three independent branches – the legislative branch (Article I), which is responsible for making federal law; the executive branch (Article II), which is responsible for enforcing national law; and the judicial branch (Article III), which applies and interprets federal (but also state) law by resolving disputes between parties in conflict.

1.   Separation of powers: an overview of the federal government

The constitutional design provides for a separation of governmental powers by the creation of three independent and co-equal branches of government, as described below.

a.   Article I: The U.S. Congress

Article I of the United States Constitution establishes the U.S. Congress as the national legislature, and proclaims that «[a]ll legislative Powers herein granted shall be vested in a Congress of the United States.»

(1)   Two chambers

Congress consists of two chambers – a House of Representatives and a Senate. Although the two chambers are on an equal footing in terms of their role in the law-making processes, the Senate is widely regarded as the higher chamber of Congress.

(a)   The House of Representatives

Members of the House of Representatives are elected from congressional districts within each state. There are 435 members of the House of Representatives, a number that is set by statute and apportioned on the basis of the population of each state. Members of the House of Representatives must be at least 25 years of age, must have been a citizen of the United States for at least seven (7) years, and must live in the state from which elected. Representatives are elected directly by the people who live within the congressional district that they seek to represent, serve two-year terms, and are eligible to run for an unlimited number of terms.

The presiding officer of the House of Representatives is the Speaker of the House. The Speaker is a member of the House and is elected by its members. The House has the power to originate all bills for raising revenue, i.e., taxation bills. The House also holds the power of impeachment (the bringing up on charges) of federal officers, including the President, Vice-President, and federal judges.

(b)   The Senate

Each state elects two Senators for a total of 100 Senators. Senators must be at least 30 years of age, must have been a citizen of the United States for nine (9) years, and must live in the state from which elected. Pursuant to the Seventeenth Amendment, Senators are elected directly by the people of each state. Senators serve six-year terms, subject to re-election for an unlimited number of terms.

The Vice-President of the United States is the President of the Senate and presides over Senate activities. The Vice-President votes in the Senate only in the event of a tie. The Senate is responsible for confirming presidential nominations of federal judges, members of the President's cabinet, and ambassadors and consuls to foreign countries. The Senate is also responsible for ratifying international treaties and for the trial of impeached officials.

(2)   Congress as a non-parliamentary body

Congress does not operate as a parliamentary body, and there is no requirement or expectation that the political party of the President holds a majority in either chamber of Congress. (The United States is essentially a two-party system.) Indeed, it is often the case that one or both chambers of Congress is not controlled by the party of the President.

(3)   The legislative process

Members of the Senate and the House of Representatives can introduce legislation in their respective chambers. Proposed legislation is called a «bill,» and bills are often introduced simultaneously in both chambers. Even within a single chamber, it is not unusual for a bill to have several sponsors.

Each chamber of Congress is organized into committees based on subject matter. Committees are then divided into sub-committees. The committees and sub-committees are enormously important to the work of the U.S Congress: They undertake hearings, research, and other fact investigation; and perform oversight of government actors within their subject matter. These committees and sub-committees are also active in the drafting of legislation and may substantially modify proposed legislation that is sent to them for consideration. Committees and sub-committees may push the vote of a bill forward to the full floor or may in effect defeat legislation by not recommending that it be placed for a vote on the floor of the Senate or House chamber. The chair of each committee and sub-committee is a member of the majority party in that chamber, and important committee and sub-committee chairs are desirable and influential positions.

To become law, legislation must be passed by a majority vote in both chambers. The proposed legislation is then sent to the President of the United States for his approval. If the President signs the bill, it becomes law. The President may also veto legislation. A veto is accompanied by a message indicating the President's reasons for refusing to sign the legislation. In the event of a veto, the proposed bill will not become law unless the veto is overridden by a two-thirds majority in both the Senate *and* the House of Representatives. Finally, the President may instead neither sign the bill nor veto it, in which case the bill will become law after ten days (excluding Sundays), unless Congress has adjourned before the ten days have elapsed. This is known as a «pocket veto.»

(4)   Limits on federal legislative power

Article I delineates the areas within which Congress may act. Central to the notion of federalism, Congress has limited powers. These powers are enumerated in Article I section 8. For the most part, powers conferred on Congress are those that one would expect a national government to have, especially those as to which national uniformity is particularly desirable. Thus, Congress is authorized to «lay and collect Taxes, Duties, Imposts, and Excises, to pay the Debts and provide for the common Defence,» to «borrow money on the credit of the United States,» to establish uniform rules on bankruptcy and naturalization, to coin money, to fix a standard of weights and measures, to develop copyright and patent laws, to establish and control post offices, to govern the District of Columbia (the seat of the federal government), and to declare war. Congress is also empowered to create federal courts below the United States Supreme Court.

There are a few aspects of Article I section 8 that have led to difficulty in determining those activities that are appropriate for Congressional action and those that are not. Notably, the third provision of Article I section 8, which allows Congress to regulate «commerce... among the several states,» has given the courts a good deal of trouble. The interpretation of this provision, known as the «interstate commerce clause,» has changed somewhat over time.

The interstate commerce clause gives Congress some of its most important powers, including broad power to regulate the economy and business. The Supreme Court has interpreted the term «commerce» to include not only trade but other kinds of commercial activity, and includes not only transactions across state lines but also any activity that «substantially affects» interstate commerce. Nevertheless, the question what activities fall within Congress's commerce clause authority remains unclear and has been the subject of several highly divisive Supreme Court decisions in recent years.

The commerce clause also carries with it the implication, long established by case law, that states may not regulate interstate commerce, absent Congressional consent. Under this rule, known as the «dormant commerce clause» or the «negative commerce clause,» states cannot through tariffs or other discriminatory practices create barriers to trade of out of state goods or services. The commerce clause thus was intended to create a free trade zone within the United States.

The other provision of Article I section 8 that has given the courts pause is the final clause, which enables Congress to make all laws «that shall be necessary and proper for carrying into execution the foregoing Powers and all other Powers vested by this Constitution in the Government of the United States, or in any Department or Officer thereof.» Known as the «necessary and proper» or the «elastic» clause because of its ability to stretch, this provision allows Congress to regulate broadly within its areas of delegated authority.

Under the interstate commerce clause and the necessary and proper clause, Congress has been able to claim expansive, although not unlimited, powers that are not explicitly authorized in the Constitution.

Finally, it bears noting that Congress's power to spend coupled with its power to «provide for the common Defence and general Welfare of the United States» has been expansively interpreted to give Congress the power to regulate areas through conditions on spending that it might not be able to regulate directly.

(5)   The non-delegation doctrine

Article I section 1 begins with the following prescription: «All legislative Powers herein granted shall be vested in a Congress of the United States...» This provision has been interpreted to mean that Congress may not delegate its lawmaking powers, a principle that has become known as the «non-delegation» doctrine. The United States Congress, however, tends to draft legislation broadly, with direction given to an administrative agency to develop rules and regulations that add detail to the contours established by Congress through legislation.

Apparently in recognition of Congress's institutional limitations, the Supreme Court has given quite a bit of leeway to Congress under this provision and will uphold delegations by Congress as long as the legislation sets forth an «intelligible principle» to which the agency is directed to conform. Such an «intelligible principle» has been found in statutes in which Congress directed that enforcement be consistent with norms as vague and broad as «necessary to avoid an imminent hazard to the public safety,» avoidance of «unduly or unnecessarily complicated» rules, avoidance of «unfair or inequitable» results, «generally fair and equitable,» those that «effectuate the purposes of [the] act,» and those that «in the public interest.»

b. Article II: The federal executive

Article II of the United States Constitution establishes the federal executive branch. Article II section I provides that the executive power «shall be vested in a President of the United States of America.» The President is elected every four years and may be elected for no more than two terms. The Constitution also establishes minimal qualifications for President – a person must be a natural born citizen of the United States, at least thirty-five years of age, and a resident of the United States for at least fourteen (14) years.

Once elected, the President selects a cabinet, each member of which must be confirmed by a majority vote of the Senate. The members of the cabinet are the President's closest advisors and include the heads of the executive departments – the Secretaries of Agriculture, Commerce, Defense, Education, Energy, Health and Human Resources, Homeland Security, Housing and Urban Development, Interior, Labor, State, Transportation, Treasury, and Veteran Affairs; and the Attorney General. Under President George W. Bush, cabinet-level rank has also been accorded to the Administrator of the Environmental Protection Agency, the Director of the Office of Management and Budget, the Director of the National Drug Control Policy, and the U.S. Trade Representative.

In addition to the departments and agencies that form the President's cabinet, there are a large number of so-called «independent agencies» that are headed by bi– partisan boards or commissions.

The President, his cabinet, members of the executive branch departments, and independent agencies are responsible for executing, or carrying out, a vast array of laws passed by Congress. All told, the executive branch consists of a large network of agencies that have substantial discretion in carrying out the federal laws with which they are charged with administering. Final decisions of these federal actors generally are subject to review by the federal courts.

Also included within the executive branch are some specialized subject-matter courts, appeals from which may be taken to traditional Article III federal courts (see Chapter III). These courts are: The United States Tax Court; the

United States Court of Military Appeals; and the United States Court of Veterans Appeals. The judges of these courts are not entitled to the protections of Article III judges, discussed below.

c. Article III: The federal judiciary

Article III of the U.S. Constitution establishes the federal judiciary. Article III section 1 specifies that there shall be «one supreme Court» and other «inferior Courts as Congress may from time to time ordain and establish.» Pursuant to this authority, Congress has established a network of «inferior,» or lower federal courts. The structure of the federal court system is discussed in Chapter III.

Federal court judges are nominated by the President and are confirmed upon the «Advice and Consent of the Senate» as prescribed by Article III section 2 of the Constitution. For most of the history of the United States, the Senate exercised its «Advice and Consent» power using very generous and liberal standards. But the Senate's role has become heavily politicized in recent years, and the power of «Advice and Consent» has often been used to prevent or stall presidential appointments to the federal judiciary on the basis of a nominee's political orientation.

It is interesting to note that Article III does not stipulate any qualifications in order to become a federal judge, in sharp contrast to Articles I and II, which provide for basic qualifications for members of Congress and the President. Federal court judges have overwhelmingly been lawyers, but this is not required, and there have been prominent federal judges who were not lawyers.

Consistent with principles of federalism, the power of the federal courts is limited.[4]

Article III of the Constitution provides for certain institutional assurances of judicial independence. Specifically, Article III section 1 provides that federal court judges are to hold their positions during «good Behaviour,» and that their compensation may not be reduced during their time in office. The «good Behaviour» provision has been interpreted to mean that federal judges enjoy life tenure.

There is another important respect in which federal courts have independence, and this is through their power of judicial review. In the landmark decision of *Marbury v. Madison* (1803), the Supreme Court firmly established the authority of the federal courts to review acts of the legislative and the executive branches and to declare such acts to be inconsistent with the Constitution. This power of judicial review remains a powerful check on the other branches of the federal government. This power has even been used to declare actions of the President of the United States to be unconstitutional.

---

4. See Chapter III.

2. Checks and balances

The separation of powers outlined above goes hand in hand with a system of checks and balances under which each branch is required to work with the other branches to carry out its functions. This system allows each branch to ensure that the other branches act within their constitutionally prescribed limits and that no single branch accumulates an excess of power.

The Constitution establishes a number of checks and balances exercised by each branch over the others. Some examples are shown in the chart that follows.

Examples of Checks and Balances in the Federal System

	Legislative Branch	Executive Branch	Judicial Branch
Checks and Balances over Legislative Branch		• Recommend legislation. • Veto power over legislation. • Policy control of agencies.	• Interpret acts of Congress. • Declare acts of Congress to be unconstitutional.
Checks and Balances over Executive Branch	• Override presidential veto. • Budgetary control. • Oversight of administrative agencies. • Confirm presidential appointments (Senate.) • Ratify treaties (Senate.) • Impeach President and executive officers (House.) • Try impeached officers (Senate.)		• Declare actions of executive to be unconstitutional. • Declare actions of executive to be inconsistent with statutory authority.
Checks and Balances over Judicial Branch	• Approve judicial nominees (Senate.) • Impeach federal judges (House.) • Try impeached federal judges (Senate.) • Control judicial salaries and budget. • Control U.S. court structure and jurisdiction. • Modify legislation prospectively after judicial interpretation.	• Nomination of federal court judges.	

B. **FEDERALISM: THE RELATIONSHIP BETWEEN STATE AND FEDERAL GOVERN-MENTS**

One of the main themes of the U.S. Constitution is federalism. Federalism is the sharing of power between or among different sovereignties – in the case of the United States, between the federal or national government and the state governments.

As discussed above, the federal government is a government of strong but limited powers – often referred to as «enumerated» powers, because the authority of the national government is limited to those aspects that are «enumerated» or listed in the Constitution. As discussed in Part A., above, the federal government has authority to regulate a wide range of activities including international affairs, interstate commerce, intellectual property, antitrust, energy and environmental issues, banks and banking, and product safety, to name a few.

Remaining governmental powers reside with the states. Each state has its own constitution and its own independent legislative, executive, and judicial branches. Indeed, there are many areas of legal life that are exclusively or primarily regulated at the state level. These include family law, tort law, contract law, corporation law, real property law, the law of inheritance and succession, and criminal law.

There are also a number of areas over which the federal and state governments have concurrent regulation. Under the Supremacy Clause of Article VI of the Constitution, valid federal law – be it constitutional, legislative, regulatory, or judicial – trumps any inconsistent state law. Whether state law is inconsistent with federal law for purposes of applying the supremacy clause can be a difficult question.

Even a state regulation that is not in conflict must give way if Congress intended that federal law should *preempt* or occupy the field. This intent may be expressly stated in the legislation or inferred from the pervasiveness of federal regulation, the need for uniformity, or the danger of conflict between concurrent federal and state regulation.

Where the line is drawn between what the federal government may regulate and what is within the exclusive province of the states is not at all a clear-cut proposition, and contentious political battles and judicial disputes on this question continue to this day.

IV.   THE AMENDMENTS: INDIVIDUAL RIGHTS AND FREEDOMS AND STRUCTURAL MODIFICATIONS

The process for amending the Constitution of the United States, outlined in Article V of the Constitution, is extremely cumbersome, and has been achieved only infrequently in the more than 200-year history of the Constitution.

There are twenty-seven amendments to the Constitution. The amendments are of two basic types – they either refine government structures and relationships, or they provide for individual rights and freedoms. Those amendments that deal with personal rights and freedoms are generally considered to be those that are most central to the development of U.S. legal culture. When amendments modify aspects of the body of the Constitution, the text of the relevant article of the Constitution itself is not changed. All amendments appear after the body of the Constitution, and the articles must be read in conjunction with any pertinent amendments.

When reading the amendments to the Constitution, as is the case with the body of the Constitution itself, it is important to remember that the meaning of these amendments has evolved over time as the Supreme Court has interpreted and applied their provisions in individual cases.

* * * *

The first ten amendments to the Constitution, known collectively as the «Bill of Rights,» were adopted in 1791. The Bill of Rights guarantees fundamental rights to the people and protects them against improper acts by the federal government. It also reinforces the limited nature of the federal government vis-à-vis the states. The Supreme Court, in specific cases decided over a number of years, has extended almost all of the protections contained in the Bill of Rights to apply as against the states (and local governments), as well. Those cases rely on the theory that those Bill of Rights protections have been «incorporated» into the due process clause of the Fourteenth Amendment, which on its face is applicable to the states.

Amendment I – The First Amendment provides for freedom of religion, freedom of speech, freedom of the press, and freedom of association. It also provides for a separation of church and state and prohibits the establishment of a national church or religion.

Amendment II – The Second Amendment has been subject to various interpretations. Some read the Second Amendment as ensuring for each state the right to maintain its own militia. Others believe that the Second Amendment gives private citizens the right to possess and carry firearms. The Supreme Court has not yet established a definitive interpretation.

Amendment III – The Third Amendment provides that soldiers may not insist on being quartered in private homes without the consent of the owner during peacetime. This amendment grew directly out of complaints against the British government, which had forced private citizens to accommodate soldiers their homes during the colonial era.

Amendment IV – The Fourth Amendment has been interpreted to require in most instances that the government obtain a search warrant issued by a judge or other neutral officer before the police can search a person or his property, seize goods, or arrest someone. In order to get such a warrant, the judge must be convinced that there is reliable evidence that a crime has been committed or is ongoing. Under the so-called «exclusionary rule» adopted by the Supreme Court, evidence obtained in violation of the Fourth Amendment may not be admitted at trial.

Amendment V – The Fifth Amendment contains a number of important protections:

- Indictment by Grand Jury – Anyone charged with a federal crime punishable by death or imprisonment must first be indicted by a grand jury. A grand jury is a special kind of jury selected to decide whether there is enough evidence against a person to maintain the charges against him. This provision has *not* been extended to the states, although many states do require indictment by a grand jury for state criminal charges.

- Prohibition on Double Jeopardy – Persons cannot be tried twice for the same offense by the same government entity. A person can be retried, however, if the jury cannot agree on a verdict (the result is called a «hung jury»), if a mistrial is declared, or if there is a remand for a new trial following a successful appeal by a convicted defendant.

- No Forced Self-Incrimination – A person cannot be forced to testify against himself or otherwise incriminate himself in criminal activity.

- Due Process – No person may be deprived of life, liberty, or property «without due process of law.» This same language appears in the Fourteenth Amendment, which is directly applicable to the states. This provision has been applied to a wide range of activities that fall into two broad categories: procedural due process and substantive due process. Due process is discussed in greater detail at the end of this section.

- Government Seizure of Property – The government may not take private property unless such a taking is: (a) for a public purpose; and (b) compensated. The right of the government to take private property for public use is known as «eminent domain.» The requirement of a «public purpose» has been given an expansive definition by the Supreme Court. Compensation is generally calculated as the fair market value of the property.

Amendment VI – The Sixth Amendment also contains several important protections for persons accused of a crime:

- Speedy and Public Trial by Jury – A person accused of a crime must be given a prompt trial that is open to the public. Such a person must have the opportunity to have the case tried before an unbiased jury composed of citizens chosen from a cross-section of the local community.[5]

- Statement of Charges – A person accused of a crime must be notified of the charges pending against him.
- Witness Confrontation – A person accused of a crime must have the opportunity to confront witnesses testifying against him. This includes the right to have the government compel the presence of witnesses that the defendant may call to testify at trial.
- Legal Representation – A person accused of a crime has the right to have a lawyer defend him at trial. If the accused cannot afford to hire a lawyer, the government must provide him with an attorney without cost.

Amendment VII – The Seventh Amendment provides for jury trials in civil suits where the amount in controversy exceeds $20. This amendment does not apply to the states, but all states also provide the right to a trial by jury in most civil cases.

Amendment VIII – The Eighth Amendment requires that bails, fines, and punishments be fair and humane and not «cruel or unusual.» Bail refers to the amount of money that a defendant must provide in a criminal case to obtain his release from custody pending trial. That amount should be enough to secure his return to court to face the charges pending against him. Although a hotly contested matter in the United States, the death penalty may be imposed if certain standards and procedural safeguards are met. A number of states still retain the penalty of death. In recent years, the Supreme Court has held that capital punishment may not be imposed on the mentally retarded or on those who were under the age of eighteen at the time the crime was committed.

Amendment IX – The Ninth Amendment was designed to make clear that the enumeration of specific rights in the Bill of Rights did not mean that other rights that were not listed were not protected.

Amendment X – The Tenth Amendment was adopted to affirm the sovereignty of the states. As such, it provides that rights not specifically given to the national government are retained by the states and/or the people. This is a clarification of the limited nature of the federal government as established by Article I, Article II, and Article III of the Constitution.

* * * *

Amendment XI (1798) – The Eleventh Amendment stipulates that a citizen of one state cannot sue another state in federal court. The Supreme Court has said that state sovereign immunity is much broader than the limited immunity offered by the Eleventh Amendment.

---

5. See Chapter VI, *infra*.

Amendment XII (1804) – The Twelfth Amendment provides that members of the electoral college (*electors*) each vote for one person as President and for another as Vice President. This amendment avoids the problem under the original election rules that could result in the President and Vice President being members of different political parties.

* * * *

The Thirteenth, Fourteenth, and Fifteenth Amendments to the U.S. Constitution are known collectively as the «Reconstruction Amendments» because they were enacted after and in response to the U.S. Civil War, when the process of «reconstructing» the nation was underway.

Amendment XIII (1865) – The Thirteenth Amendment completed the abolition of slavery in the United States. This is the only provision of the U.S. Constitution that implicates private action; all other aspects of the Constitution require or limit *government* action.

Amendment XIV (1868) – The Fourteenth Amendment is one of the most significant constitutional amendments in the post Bill of Rights era. This amendment makes former slaves and other black people citizens of both the United States and the state in which they reside. It also protects such people from state-imposed discrimination. The Fourteenth Amendment thus contains the language that states may not «deny to any person within its jurisdiction the equal protection of the laws.» The equal protection clause, as it is known, has been substantially extended to apply to the *federal* government by a process of «reverse incorporation» into the due process clause of the Fifth Amendment. Equal protection principles are discussed at the end of this chapter.

The Fourteenth Amendment contains «due process of law» language that mirrors that in the Fifth Amendment, and is discussed in greater detail below.

The provision that «Congress shall have the power to enforce, by appropriate legislation,» the Fourteenth Amendment, is the basis for much of the civil rights legislation in the United States.

Amendment XV (1870) – The Fifteenth Amendment guarantees to former slaves and other black citizens the right to vote. This amendment also gives Congress the power to enforce voting rights by «appropriate legislation.» Efforts by some southern states to deprive their black citizens of the right to vote led to the passage of federal voting rights legislation.

* * * *

Amendment XVI (1913) – The Sixteenth Amendment allows Congress to levy an income tax directly on individuals, without apportionment among the states.

Amendment XVII (1913) – The Seventeenth Amendment changed the system of voting Senators to a direct vote by the citizens of each state. Prior to this amendment, Senators were elected by the legislators of each state.

Amendment XVIII (1919) – The Eighteenth Amendment prohibited the production, sale, and transportation of liquor within the United States. This amendment was repealed by the Twenty-First Amendment.

Amendment XIX (1920) – The Nineteenth Amendment prohibits states from denying the right to vote to women.

Amendment XX (1933) – The Twentieth Amendment moves the date that newly elected presidents and members of Congress take office to closer to election time. This amendment was designed to minimize the time that officials who were not re-elected for another term («lame duck» officials) would remain in office.

Amendment XXI (1933) – The Twenty-First Amendment repeals the Eighteenth Amendment.

Amendment XXII (1951) – The Twenty-Second Amendment provides that no person can be elected to the office of president more than twice. This amendment was proposed and ratified as a reaction to the presidency of Franklin Delano Roosevelt, which lasted for four terms.

Amendment XXIII (1961) – The Twenty-Third Amendment allows the citizens of the District of Columbia to vote in presidential elections.

Amendment XXIV (1964) – The Twenty-Fourth Amendment forbids any state from imposing a tax on individuals as a pre-condition to exercising the right to vote. A number of states had used taxes as a means of keeping poor people from voting.

Amendment XXV (1967) – The Twenty-Fifth Amendment provides for succession in the event of death or disability of the president. In such a case, the vice president becomes president (in the case of the president's death) or acting president (in the case of disability). When there is a vacancy in the office of the vice president, the president appoints a vice president, subject to confirmation by a majority of both chambers of Congress.

Amendment XXVI (1971) – The Twenty-Sixth Amendment forbids states from denying the vote to citizens because of their age if they are 18 years of age or older.

Amendment XXVII (1992) – The Twenty-Seventh Amendment ensures that members of Congress cannot vote to raise their own pay. Any legislation to increase congressional pay would not take effect until after a congressional election. This amendment was approved by Congress in 1789 and was not ratified by the requisite number of states for more than 200 years.

* * * *

Concepts of due process and equal protection embraced by the Fifth Amendment and the Fourteenth Amendment to the Constitution, as described above, are enormously important in U.S. law, and thus will be discussed separately here.

Due Process

Due process is guaranteed both by the Fifth Amendment and the Fourteenth Amendment to the U.S. Constitution. There are two kinds of due process – substantive due process and procedural due process.

Substantive due process considers the constitutionality of the *substance* of a particular legal rule, and evaluates the compatibility of a law or other government action with constitutional rights. Substantive due process issues are normally implicated only when dealing with government action that affects fundamental rights and liberties, such as first amendment rights, the right to engage in interstate travel, the right to vote, the right to marry and raise a family, and the right to privacy. The courts will insist that the government prove that restrictions on such rights are *necessary* to promote a *compelling* or overriding public interest. On the other hand, legislation affecting economic or social interests will be upheld as long as the legislation bears a *rational relation* to a *legitimate* government objective.

Substantive Due Process Framework for Analysis

Right at Issue	Test Applied – Showing of Government Interest Needed to Limit/Deny the Right
Fundamental Right	**Strict Scrutiny** • **Necessary** • **Compelling government purpose** • **Burden on government**
No Fundamental Right	**Rational Basis Scrutiny** • **Rational relation** • **Legitimate government purpose** • **Burden on challenger**

Procedural due process requires that procedural safeguards to ensure fairness must accompany any government action that threatens a deprivation of *life, liberty, or property* interests. The threshold question in a procedural due process inquiry thus is whether a life, liberty, or property interest exists. The courts have interpreted liberty interests to include freedom from physical restraint and the ability to engage in freedom of action and choice regarding personal issues. Property rights include all forms of real and personal property, and certain entitlements conferred by government. The importance of procedural due process rights is perhaps best summed up by Justice Frankfurter, who once said that «[t]he history of liberty has largely been the history of procedural safeguards.»

The nature of the procedural protections that must be provided will depend on a balancing of three factors: the importance of the individual life, liberty, or property interest involved; the adequacy of existing procedural protections and the likely value of additional safeguards; and the government's interests, including interests in fiscal and administrative efficiency.

Equal Protection

The doctrine of equal protection stands for the basic proposition that the government must provide similar treatment to similarly – situated persons. A specific mandate to the states in the Fourteenth Amendment, the doctrine of equal protection also limits the federal government through the process of reverse incorporation of equal protection principles into the due process provision of the Fifth Amendment. An equal protection inquiry comes into play whenever governmental action involves the classification of people, as it often does. Whether a particular governmental classification violates the equal protection mandate depends on the nature of the right involved and/or the basis for the classification made.

When a fundamental right or a suspect classification – race or national origin – is implicated, the courts will apply strict scrutiny; under such a test, the government must show that the classification is *necessary* to promote a *compelling* or overriding governmental interest. When the government draws a line based on gender, age, or legitimacy, intermediate scrutiny is applied, and the classification must have a *substantial relation* to an *important* governmental purpose. For other legislation, for instance economic regulation, all that is required is that the classification bear a *rational* relationship to a *legitimate* governmental interest that the classification purports to further.

Equal Protection Framework for Analysis

Classification	Test Applied – Showing of Government Interest Needed to Make Distinctions Among Persons
Fundamental Right	Strict Scrutiny • Necessary • Compelling government purpose • Burden on government
Suspect Class • Race • National Origin	Strict Scrutiny • Necessary • Compelling government purpose • Burden on government
Quasi-Suspect Class • Age • Gender • Legitimacy	Intermediate Scrutiny • Substantial Relation • Important government purpose • Burden usually on government

Classification	Test Applied – Showing of Government Interest Needed to Make Distinctions Among Persons
No Suspect/Quasi-Suspect Class No fundamental right	**Rational Basis Scrutiny** • **Rational relation** • **Legitimate government purpose** • **Burden on challenger**

CHAPTER III

U.S. JUDICIAL SYSTEMS

I. INTRODUCTION AND OVERVIEW

It is not accurate to speak of a single judicial system in the United States. Judicial systems in the U.S. include the federal court system and independent judicial systems in each state. Federal courts and state courts constitute parallel and sovereign systems. Other than in a few specific situations, a case will go *either* through the federal court system or through a state court system. A case normally does not go from one judicial system to another.

The focus of this discussion will be on the federal judicial system. Most state court systems are similar in structure to the federal system, but some important differences will be discussed at the end of this chapter.

Under Article III section 3, federal courts are empowered to hear only «cases or controversies,» which means that the federal courts are not authorized to issue advisory opinions. Federal courts may interpret law only through the resolution of actual legal disputes brought to them by parties with a real interest in the outcome of the dispute. Courts cannot address hypothetical issues, nor can they resolve matters on their own initiative. Under what is known as the doctrine of «standing,» the plaintiff must establish a «concrete and particularized harm» rather than some «generalized grievance» in order to bring a case in federal court. And the case must not have become moot – in other words, the case must present an ongoing problem for the court to resolve. State courts have similar limitations.

The fact that courts in the United States will not give advisory opinions is closely related to the adversarial nature of the U.S. legal system, which is explored in some detail in Chapter VI. Because courts rely so heavily on the parties acting as adversaries, and because court decisions serve as precedent – often binding – in subsequent cases, judicial decisions should be made only in situations in which the parties can be counted on to bring to the court the highest level of committed advocacy consistent with ethical standards.

II. FEDERAL COURTS

A. CONSTITUTIONAL BASIS AND STRUCTURE

Article III section 1 of the U.S. Constitution establishes the judicial branch. Specifically, the Constitution provides that «[t]he judicial Power of the United

States, shall be vested in one supreme Court, and in such inferior Courts as the Congress may from time to time ordain and establish.»

The framers considered an independent judiciary to be essential to our legal system. The Constitution thus includes several institutional mechanisms designed to preserve the independence of the federal judiciary. First, the Constitution provides that federal judges serve «during good Behaviour,» a provision that has always been interpreted to mean that federal court judges hold life tenure subject only to impeachment and removal from office for conviction of «high crimes and misdemeanors.» The Constitution also provides that judicial salaries may not be reduced, further insulating federal court judges from political pressure.

Perhaps even more critical to judicial independence is the separation of powers between the branches of the federal government that characterizes our Constitutional framework. This separation of powers ensures that the judiciary operates with the requisite independence. One especially important product of the independence of the judiciary is the power of judicial review by which courts may review acts of its sister branches and of state governments to ensure compliance with the Constitution and other federal laws.

The Constitution provides that federal judges are appointed upon the nomination of the President and confirmation by the Senate. There is no separate career track for federal judges, and most judges do not enter the judiciary until having some, and in many cases a significant number of years of law practice in the public or private sector. Somewhat curiously, the Constitution does not provide any minimal qualifications that a person needs to possess in order to be a federal judge. This is especially odd given that the Constitution does specify qualifications for members of the Congress and the President. Perhaps the drafters of the Constitution thought that the involvement of both the President and the Senate in the selection of federal judges would be sufficient safeguard for the appointment of well-qualified individuals.

B.   OVERVIEW OF FEDERAL COURT STRUCTURE

The federal court system in the United States is based on a hierarchical and a geographical organization of courts. The federal court system resembles a pyramid – at the base of this system are the district courts, which are the primary trial-level courts; just above the district courts is the court of appeals; at the apex of the federal court system is the nation's highest court – the Supreme Court of the United States.

The federal courts are courts of *general* jurisdiction. This means that, with a very few exceptions discussed below, the federal courts are not specialized courts; all federal courts are authorized to hear a variety of cases that may deal with civil matters, criminal matters, and matters of federal constitutional or statutory law. But at the same time, the federal courts are courts of *limited* jurisdiction, which means that they have authority to hear only certain kinds of cases.[1]

The rulings of the United States Supreme Court on matters of federal law are binding on every court in the country. Under the level of the Supreme Court, the federal courts are divided into circuits, most of which are organized geographically. Such a circuit consists of the court of appeals for that circuit and all district courts located within the geographic boundary of that circuit. This geographic and hierarchical division of courts in the federal system is of critical importance because rules of *stare decisis* – the extent to which a court must follow rulings established in other cases[2] – is largely informed by the geographic and hierarchical distribution of courts. A map showing circuit and district boundaries is found in Appendix II.

1.   United States District Courts

The United States district courts are the principal trial courts in the federal court system. Most federal cases begin at the trial court level. With the exception of the few specialized federal courts and some appeals from final agency action which by statute go directly to the court of appeals, the district courts have jurisdiction to hear almost every category of federal cases.

Congress has divided the nation into 94 judicial districts, each of which has one district court. Each state has one or more judicial districts, depending on the size and population of the state. There is also one judicial district each for the District of Columbia, for Puerto Rico, and for the overseas territories. The number of judges in each district varies depending on the population and the amount of judicial business of the district.

Each federal judicial district includes a United States bankruptcy court that operates as a unit of the district court. The bankruptcy court has jurisdiction over almost all matters involving insolvency issues. Judges of the bankruptcy court are appointed for terms of fourteen years. Each district court also has a number of magistrate judges. Federal magistrate judges hold hearings on non-dispositive motions, conduct trials with the consent of the parties, and make recommended decisions for review by a district court judge. Magistrate judges are selected by district court judges from a list provided by a screening committee of lawyers and non-lawyers, and serve terms of eight years. Bankruptcy judges and magistrate judges thus do not enjoy the benefits of lifetime tenure enjoyed by «Article III» judges.

The federal court system also includes two special courts at the trial level. The Court of International Trade hears cases involving international trade and customs issues. The United States Court of Federal Claims has jurisdiction

---

1.   Subject matter jurisdiction is discussed in greater detail later in this chapter.
2.   See Chapter V, *infra*.

over disputes involving federal contracts, the taking of private property by the federal government, and a variety of other monetary claims against the United States. Both courts have nationwide jurisdiction over the matters within their jurisdiction.

Trial court proceedings are conducted by a single judge, usually with a jury of citizens as finders of fact. A very small number of federal statutes specify trials by a panel of three judges, usually with direct mandatory review by the United States Supreme Court.

The end product of a trial court decision is a verdict, normally issued by a jury.[3] The verdict is entered into the record by the trial court judge but without any formal opinion. Trial court decisions on motions may be published.

2.   United States Court of Appeals

The 94 judicial districts are organized into twelve (12) regional circuits, each of which has one United States Court of Appeals. A court of appeals hears appeals from the district courts located within that circuit. Appeals may also be brought directly to the court of appeals from decisions issued by federal administrative agencies, when provided for by statute; this is because the administrative agency has already undergone a fact-finding process and there is thus no need for a district court to perform that same function.

There is one specialized federal appellate court – the Court of Appeals for the Federal Circuit. This court has nationwide jurisdiction to hear appeals from cases decided by the Court of International Trade and the Court of Federal Claims.

There is a right of appeal in every federal case in which a district court has entered final judgment. The federal court of appeals typically sits in panels of three judges. Decisions are made primarily on the basis of briefs, which are written submissions by the parties arguing that the lower court did or did not commit reversible legal error (depending on the party's position in the appeal). The court of appeals also often orders the parties to appear for oral argument. The court of appeals generally does not revisit factual findings made below and does not hear evidence. Appeals are limited to claims of legal error below.

Most court of appeals decisions are formally issued in writing and many are published, although there is a growing trend on the part of the court of appeals to issue unpublished decisions. Unpublished decisions may not be cited as precedent in future cases and are considered to be binding only on the parties to that particular case. There is an ongoing debate as to the appropriateness of issuing unpublished opinions.

---

3. See Chapter VI, *infra.*

3. Supreme Court of the United States

The Supreme Court of the United States is the highest court in the federal judiciary. There are nine justices on the Supreme Court – the Chief Justice and eight associate justices. The Supreme Court sits *en banc* and all nine justices participate in all cases to come before the court, unless one of the justices recuses himself or herself, for example, to avoid a potential conflict of interest.

The jurisdiction of the Supreme Court can roughly be divided between its *original* jurisdiction and its *appellate* jurisdiction. The Court's appellate jurisdiction, in turn, can be divided between *mandatory* appellate jurisdiction and *discretionary* appellate jurisdiction, also known as *certiorari* jurisdiction.

The Supreme Court of the United States has a very small area of original jurisdiction over cases between states and cases «involving ambassadors, other public ministers and consuls.» These cases are heard by the Supreme Court sitting as a court of first instance.

The Court's appellate jurisdiction is much broader and includes the power – and in some cases the obligation – to review cases.

In a very small number of cases, Congress has provided for mandatory appellate jurisdiction in the Supreme Court. Many of these mandatory appeals are brought directly from a district court.

The overwhelming majority of cases that reach the Supreme Court do so by way of the Court's discretionary appellate jurisdiction under its *certiorari* review. A petition for a writ of *certiorari* is submitted by a party aggrieved by the lower court decision to be reviewed. If four of the nine members of the Court agree to hear the case, the writ of *certiorari* will be granted. The Court generally agrees to accept only cases of great national importance, with the goal of national uniformity being particularly important. The Supreme Court receives some 8,000 petitions for a writ of *certiorari* each term (the Court's term begins in early October and typically concludes at the end of the following June or the begining of July), only about 100 of which are granted. When the Court declines to grant the writ, it does not provide a reason; and denials of the writ of *certiorari* may not be treated as precedent as to the Court's view of the legal issue presented.

The Court reaches decisions on cases before it through written briefs submitted by the parties and, in most cases, after oral argument. The justices then meet privately to discuss the cases and take a preliminary vote. At that point, one of the justices is assigned to draft the opinion on behalf of the majority of the members of the Court. The Chief Justice assigns the task of writing the majority opinion if he is in the majority; he may assign it to himself or to one of the other justices in the majority. If the Chief Justice is not in the majority, the opinion writing assignment is made by the most senior associate justice in the majority. Other justices draft and circulate amongst thenselves dissenting and concurring opinions.

Decisions of the United States Supreme Court on questions of federal law are final and may not be reversed, except that: (1) The Supreme Court itself may overrule its own decisions in subsequent cases; (2) When a Supreme Court decision is based on the U.S. Constitution, the Constitution can be amended to change the effect of the Court's decision prospectively; and (3) When a Supreme Court decision is based on a statute, Congress can amend the statute to change the prospective effect of the Court's decision. Nevertheless, as explored in Chapter V, Court decisions often leave room for differing interpretations by lower courts.

C. ADMINISTRATION OF THE FEDERAL COURT SYSTEM

Each federal court judge has a number of *clerks*, as prescribed by statute. Federal court clerkships are extremely competitive, and these positions are normally held by the top graduates of the top U.S. law schools. The overwhelming majority of clerkships are for limited time periods, generally one or two years, although some judges retain one or more «permanent» law clerks because they prefer the stability that such clerks provide.

The federal courts are largely decentralized with a «bottom up» rather than a «top down» management organization. Each district court and each court of appeals has its own administrative structure. Each court has a *chief judge*, determined by seniority, except that a judge cannot be chief judge after the age of 70. In addition to presiding over cases, the chief judge handles the court's administrative matters. However, the chief judge has no special authority to influence the outcome of cases in that court. The chief judge has only one vote, votes only in cases to which he is assigned, and cannot veto the votes of other judges.

Each district court and court of appeals has a *clerk of court*. The clerk is the court's chief administrative officer. The clerk's office is responsible for the docketing and processing of cases, managing the court's budget and personnel, and providing information to the public. The clerk's office also administers the trial court's jury system and provides interpreters and court reporters and other courtroom support services.

Each circuit has a *circuit judicial council* made up of an equal number of circuit and district court judges. The chief judge of that circuit's court of appeals is the presiding officer. Each council is charged by Congress with «the effective and expeditious administration of justice within each circuit.» Each circuit has a *circuit executive* who is responsible for all non-judicial activities of the circuit. The circuit executive also performs a range of administrative duties at the request of the chief judge and acts as secretary of the judicial council.

The *Chief Justice of the United States* is the head of the federal judiciary. The Chief Justice has a small staff headed by an Administrative Assistant who is selected by and serves at the pleasure of the Chief Justice.

The *Judicial Conference of the United States* is the policy-making body of the federal courts. The Chief Justice of the United States presides over and chairs the conference, which meets twice per year. The Judicial Conference operates largely through committees composed primarily of judges from throughout the federal system. Some committees include a small number of government officials, lawyers, and law professors in their membership. The Judicial Conference is charged with recommending changes in the federal rules of procedure, formulating guidelines on judicial ethics, and communicating with Congress about proposed legislation that affects the federal courts.

The *Administrative Office of the United States Courts* is the administrative arm of the federal courts. It reports to and carries out the policy decisions of the Judicial Conference. It is also responsible for collecting and analyzing court statistics and other data and for administering the federal courts' budget.

The *Federal Judicial Center* is the research and education agency for the federal courts. Its functions include sponsoring educational programs for judges and other court employees.

III.   CHOOSING A COURT: JURISDICTION AND RELATED ISSUES

There are numerous issues that must be determined when deciding the court in which to file a lawsuit. These include (A) subject matter jurisdiction; (B) venue; and (C) personal jurisdiction; and the related issue of (D) choice of law.

A.   SUBJECT MATTER JURISDICTION: FEDERAL OR STATE COURT?

As indicated above, the federal courts are courts of *general* jurisdiction but also of *limited* jurisdiction, which means that they have authority to hear and decide only limited kinds of cases. Subject matter jurisdiction goes to the very power of a court to hear a case and involves the question whether a case can be brought in federal court or whether it must be filed in state court.

State and federal courts often have concurrent jurisdiction over cases; such cases could be brought either in federal or in state court. State courts have much broader jurisdiction than do federal courts. Any case can be brought in state court unless there is a specific federal law requiring that the case be brought in federal court.

The most important sources of federal court jurisdiction are (1) federal question jurisdiction; and (2) diversity jurisdiction. The closely related doctrines of (3) removal and supplemental jurisdiction are also discussed. When a court lacks subject matter jurisdiction, (4) the court lacks the power to do anything other than dismiss the case.

1.   Federal question jurisdiction

The federal courts have jurisdiction over questions that «arise under» federal law. Known as federal question jurisdiction, cases can be brought in the federal courts if they «arise under» federal constitutional or statutory law.

2.   Diversity jurisdiction

Under diversity jurisdiction, a case can be brought in federal court if (a) the parties are citizens of different states, or of a state and a foreign country; and (b) the amount in controversy is $75,000 or more, an amount that can be (and has been in the past) adjusted by Congress. By definition, diversity cases arise under state law rather than under federal law. Diversity jurisdiction is a response to the concern that state courts would be biased in favor of their own citizens in cases involving significant amounts of money. Thus, the federal courts will not have jurisdiction in the absence of «complete» diversity; in other words, diversity will be destroyed if there is at least one defendant of the same citizenship as any one of the paintiffs.

As to natural persons, citizenship for purposes of diversity is determined by that person's domicile, *i.e.*, his physcal presence in the state plus a present intent to reside there indefinitely. A corporation is a citizen of the state of incorporation *and* the state in which its principal place of business is located.

3.   A note about removal and supplemental jurisdiction

Under *removal jurisdiction*, if the plaintiff brings an action in state court that could have been brought in federal court, the defendant may *remove* the case to federal court. The only exception is that a defendant may not excercise removal jurisdiction if the case is based on diversity jurisdiction and the case was brought in defendant's own state court.

Under *supplemental jurisdiction*, federal courts may resolve state law matters that come before them if those matters are closely related to a federal matter to be litigated in the same case. Supplemental jurisdiction is based on efficiencies for the parties and the legal system generally of hearing related state and federal law claims together in a single proceeding.

4.   Effect of a lack of subject matter jurisdiction

Because subject matter jurisdiction goes to the competency of a court to hear and decide a case before it, lack of subject matter jurisdiction may not be waived by the parties or ignored by the court. If a federal court decides that it does not have subject matter jurisdiction over a case before it, it will dismiss the case, and the plaintiff will have to re-file in state court. Objections to a court's subject matter jurisdiction can be raised at any time in the proceedings, including on appeal, and may also be raised by the court *sua sponte* (on its own motion).

B. PERSONAL JURISDICTION

Once the question of subject matter jurisdiction is resolved and it has been decided whether a case will go to federal or state court, the question then arises as to *which* federal or state court should entertain the case. This involves preliminarily the question which court or courts have *personal jurisdiction* over the defendant – whether a particular court has the authority to compel the presence of an out-of-state defendant. (The question of personal jurisdiction over the plaintiff does not arise because the plaintiff is considered to have acquiesced to the jurisdiction of the court in which he chose to file a lawsuit.)

Personal jurisdiction does not go to the actual authority of a court to hear a particular matter but instead goes to the authority of a court to require the defendant to appear in that court. Personal jurisdiction thus can be waived by a defendant. In fact, a defendant that does not object to personal jurisdiction in his first appearance or filing before the court will be deemed to have waived any objection to personal jurisdiction and the case can proceed against him.

The question of personal jurisdiction is a two-part inquiry. First, the court needs to look at the long-arm statute of the state in which it sits. If the long-arm statute gives rise to personal jurisdiction over the defendant, then the court needs to consider whether compelling the presence of the defendant in that court would violate due process concerns.

1. State long-arm statute

Each state has a long arm statute that prescribes situations under which a person residing outside of the state may be brought into a court as a defendant in that jurisdiction. If a defendant does not fall within the reach of the state's long arm statute, then he may not be required to defend a lawsuit there. If a defendant's presence in the state is permitted by the statute, then the court continues on to the due process issue. Often, state long arm statutes permit courts to compel the presence in court in that state of any defendant whose presence does not violate due process concerns. In such situations, the court will go directly to an analysis of due process issues.

2. Due process

The Supreme Court of the United States has set forth a test for whether due process principles are violated when bringing an out-of-state defendant into a state for the purposes of answering a lawsuit. Under this test, the defendant must have «minimal purposeful contacts with the forum state so as not to offend fundamental notions of fair play and justice.» This inquiry may be relatively simple at times and at other times rather complicated.

C.   VENUE

There may be several courts in which both subject matter jurisdiction and personal jurisdiction are appropriate. The plaintiff must pick one of the locales where the court has both personal and subject matter jurisdiction as the location in which to file the lawsuit. This geographic choice is called a question of «venue.» General principles behind venue selection are convenience and fairness to one or more of the parties and efficiency for the court.

Venue is sometimes prescribed by statute for particular types of cases. For example, venue in cases involving real estate is generally where property is located. In other cases, venue may be proper where the cause of action arose; where a particular fact or situation occurred; where the defendant resides or has a place of business; where the plaintiff resides or has a place of business; where the defendant is served with a complaint; or where the seat of government is located.

A defendant may make a motion to dismiss a cause of action for lack of proper venue, but this objection will be waived if the defendant does not make it in his first appearance before the court. The defendant may also move that venue be changed to a more convenient forum (*forum non conveniens*), for example to a place where more of the witnesses, documents, etc., are located. Unlike objections to subject matter jurisdiction, the issue of venue is not one of constitutional import, and will not be raised by the court on its own motion.

D.   CHOICE OF LAW

Once a court has been selected for litigation, that court must determine which law to apply. Choice of law is complicated by the fact that, as discussed above, issues of state law may be adjudicated in federal court, and *vice versa*. In addition, state courts may be called upon to decide matters of federal law or the law of another state.

Choice of law involves two separate questions – choice of law on *procedural* matters and choice of law as to *substantive* matters. These rules are the product of a series of cases decided by the U.S. Supreme Court beginning with *Erie Railroad Co. v. Tompkins* (1938), and known as the *Erie* rule.

1.   Procedural matters

A court will apply its own procedural rules regardless of the type of case that is before it or the basis upon which its jurisdiction is grounded. Thus, federal courts will apply federal procedural rules, and state courts will apply that state's procedural rules.

Federal procedural laws include the Federal Rules of Civil Procedure, the Federal Rules of Evidence, the Federal Rules of Criminal Procedure, the Federal Rules of Appellate Procedure, the Rules of the Supreme Court of the United States, and a number of rules at the circuit and district court levels. Individual judges may also have their own rules that are applicable in cases before them.

2.   Substantive matters

Choice of law questions as to substantive matters tend to be a bit more complex. Substantive choice of law questions turn on the underlying cause of action involved. If the underlying cause of action is premised on federal law, then the court will need to look to and apply federal substantive law in resolving it. In doing so, the court will consider precedent and rules of *stare decisis* as explored more fully in Chapter V. If the case arises under state law, then the court must apply substantive state law. But which state law? This can be a controversial issue and the parties often argue about which state substantive law applies. The court will usually apply the substantive law of the state in which the cause of action arose or the state with the most significant contacts and/or interest in the litigation. A court's decision as to which law to apply may be an extremely complex endeavor.

When a federal court is sitting in diversity or when a state court is called upon to apply the law of another state, that court must «stand in the shoes» of the highest state court to decide how it would rule. If that court has decisively resolved the issue at hand, that is normally the end of the inquiry and the court must apply the decision of the state high court. There may be some room to maneuver in such a case in which the high court decision is old, has not been revisited in some time, and seems otherwise inconsistent with other high court rulings on related or analogous issues.

IV.   SOME NOTES ABOUT STATE COURT SYSTEMS

A.   AUTONOMOUS AND INDEPENDENT SYSTEMS

Each state has its own court system that is autonomous and independent of the federal court system. These court systems are created and governed by state law, subject, of course, to due process and other restraints mandated by the Constitution of the United States.

The state court of last resort is the ultimate authority on the interpretation of the law of that state. As noted above, federal courts and other state courts interpreting and applying state law are to «stand in the shoes» of the state court of last resort and apply the law as it thinks the state court would.

At least 90% of all civil and criminal litigation in the United Sates is conducted in the courts of one of the 50 states or of the District of Columbia. These courts dispose of about fourteen million disputes each year. These include a range of important kinds of cases, including family matters, criminal proceedings, contact disputes and other commercial matters, property disputes, and probate and inheritance issues.

B.   STRUCTURE OF STATE COURT SYSTEMS

Most state court systems are structured much like the federal courts, with a three-tiered structure composed of trial courts, intermediate appellate courts, and a court of last resort. The state court of last resort is usually called the state Supreme Court, but that is not always the case. In New York State, for example, the court of last resort is the New York Court of Appeals. A few of the smaller states only have one appellate court and thus have no intermediate appellate court.

State court systems also tend to have far more specialized courts than does the federal court system. Although such courts differ from jurisdiction to jurisdiction, many states have specialized courts for criminal law, family law, small claims, trust and probate matters, and commercial law.

C.   SELECTION OF STATE COURT JUDGES

State court judges are also selected in a different fashion from federal court judges and serve different terms. In the majority of states, judges are elected. Election of state court judges has been criticized on a number of grounds, including that those who vote know little about the candidates for judicial office; that elections oblige judges to engage in campaign fundraising, which strikes many as unseemly for those who would serve in a judicial role; and that judicial elections have the potential to compromise judicial independence. In some states, judges run for election on party labels, further politicizing the process.

In some states, judges are selected, often by the governor. In some such states, the governor selects judges from among a number of persons recommended by panels of lawyers. In other states, judges are named upon gubernatorial appointment with legislative consent.

CHAPTER IV

U.S. SOURCES OF LAW AND RELATED ISSUES

I. INTRODUCTION

Sources of law in the United States reflect certain fundamental aspects of American law and the U.S. legal system. *First*, the U.S. Constitution is the basis for all federal laws and is the most important and highest source of law in the United States. *Second*, U.S. sources of law reflect the vertical structure of government and principles of federalism in two respects: First, sources of law are created at both the federal and state levels; second, they reflect the principle of supremacy, under which all valid federal laws are above all state laws in the hierarchy. *Third*, U.S. sources of law reflect the horizontal structure or separation of powers within the federal and state governments, in that legal sources are derived from all three branches of government – legislative, executive, and judicial. *Finally*, American legal authorities reflect the primacy of case law that is central to the U.S. common law tradition.

II. PRIMARY VERSUS SECONDARY U.S. LEGAL AUTHORITIES

In discussing sources of law it is useful to distinguish between *primary* sources of law and *secondary* sources of law.

A. PRIMARY SOURCES OF LAW

1. Defined

Primary sources of law are normative sources of law that create rights and obligations. Simply stated, primary sources of law are *the law* – positive legal authorities that carry the force of law.

2. Primary sources of law as a reflection of federalism and separation of powers

As indicated above, primary legal authorities reflect the structure of the U.S. legal system as one embracing principles of federalism and of separation of governmental powers within individual sovereignties. Thus, primary sources include federal and state laws. This includes the government charters themselves: the U.S. Constitution, and the constitution of each of the states; legislation, or statutory law, at the federal and state levels; regulations and other administrative issuances, at both the federal and state levels; and case law, or «judge-made law,» again at the federal and state levels.

3. Hierarchy of primary sources of law

Because more than one source of law may be applicable to a particular legal situation, the relationship between individual sources of law is important. The hierarchy of primary legal authorities in a given case will include both questions of federalism and separation of powers.

Federalism – Under the Supremacy clause of Article VI of the U.S. Constitution, all valid federal laws are supreme to – and thus supersede – any conflicting state law.

Separation of powers – Within sovereignties, the constitution is the highest source of law. Below the constitution in the level of hierarchy is legislation, followed by administrative regulations and other executive branch issuances, and finally, case law.

Primary sources are generally binding within the jurisdiction where they operate, assuming that they are not inconsistent with the U.S. Constitution and, in the case of state law, not inconsistent with federal law.

Case law merits a special discussion in this regard. Some case law is binding on courts deciding similar cases in the future. Whether case law will be binding in a subsequent case is a somewhat complicated inquiry that turns on a number of factors, as discussed in Chapter V.

B. SECONDARY LEGAL AUTHORITIES

Secondary legal authorities are not the law and they do not create legal rights or obligations. Instead, they explain, discuss, interpret, outline, criticize, and/or seek changes to the law. Secondary sources thus include law review or journal articles, treatises, hornbooks, legal encyclopedias, Restatements, and other books. Model and uniform laws are also an important source of secondary authority.

Secondary authorities are never binding or mandatory, although courts may consult them in the absence of binding primary authority, or to better understand primary authority. Certain forms of secondary authorities are very useful to practitioners and courts while others are of interest mainly to academics.

1. Law review/journal articles

Every law school in the United States publishes one or more law journal, often called law reviews. There are general topic journals, for example, the *Harvard Law Journal* and the *Yale Law Review*. There are also special topic law journals, such as the *Fordham Intellectual Property, Media & Entertainment Law Journal* and the *Columbia Human Rights Law Review.*

Law journals in the United States are by and large edited by students. Staff positions are competitive, and top editorial positions even more so. Membership is generally decided by grades and/or a writing competition that takes place at the end of the first year of law school. Editorial positions are selected by the members of the staff. Student editors and staff members are responsible for selecting articles that are submitted for publication, working with the authors in editing the articles, and ensuring that the sources and citations in the articles are accurate. Many journals also sponsor symposia that become the basis for subsequent issues.

A few journals are not edited by students but by law professors. These so-called «peer edited» journals are few in number in the U.S. relative to student-edited journals.

Although law reviews are sometimes used by practitioners and cited in court decisions, journals have been criticized as being too academic and theoretical in focus and not practical enough to be useful to attorneys or judges. This assessment is perhaps most accurate as to the law reviews published by the most prestigious law schools. Law reviews are of great interest to legal academics, and publication in law journals remains essential for advancement in U.S. legal academe.

The *Index to Legal Periodicals* and the *Current Law Index* are the traditional resources for locating journal articles. Various internet resources which provide access to law journal articles are now also available on a fee-based or gratuitous basis.

2. Legal Encyclopedias/Treatises/American Law Reports

Legal encyclopedias, treatises, and the American Law Reports are general reference sources that are most useful to the researcher who has little or no background in the area of law that he or she is researching.

a. *Legal Encyclopedias*

The major legal encyclopedias are *American Jurisprudence* (known as «Am Jur») and *Corpus Juris Secundum: Complete Restatement of the Entire American Law as Developed by All Reported Cases* (known as «Corpus Juris Secundum» or «C.J.S.»), both of which are published by West.

Am Jur and *C.J.S.* are comprehensive reference works on a wide range of legal subjects, organized alphabetically. Each subject is broken down into sections, and sample case citations are provided in footnotes to the text. Am Jur and C.J.S. are multi-volume sets, but are necessarily relatively superficial in their treatment of specific issues.

Am Jur has some state-specific volumes, such as *N.Y. Jur.* (for New York) and *Cal. Jur.* (for California).

b. Treatises

Treatises are practitioner-oriented books that explain in detail the law relating to a particular subject by providing general rules and concepts. Treatises vary in depth of treatment and length. Some are single volume books, often called «hornbooks,» while others are multi-volume sets that offer much greater specificity in their treatment.

c. American Law Reports (A.L.R.)

American Law Reports (A.L.R.) is a series of reports organized by date of publication rather than thematically. A.L.R. publishes articles that are narrowly focused on discrete topics and often are based on specific court opinions. Articles will cite to all reported cases on the issue. Articles can be found by using the subject index. A.L.R. makes no pretense of being comprehensive but can be very helpful if there is an entry on a topic of interest.

3. Restatements

Restatements of the law hold a special place among U.S. legal authorities. Beginning in the early twentieth century, it was felt that it was increasingly difficult to understand trends in state laws, given the varying development in the laws of the various states, especially in fields in which case law was dominant, such as contracts, property, and torts. With this in mind, the American Law Institute (ALI) was created in 1923 in part to support the «clarification and simplification of the law.»[1]

A major project of the ALI is a series of «restatements,» which are efforts to «restate» specific areas of the law. The Restatement in each field was drafted by one or more «reporters» – eminent law teachers in collaboration with advisors, practitioners, and judges. Each restatement is divided into sections, which are black-letter statements of principles or rules, followed by comments that explain their purpose and scope, with illustrations of their application. Reporter's notes cite cases and other authorities and may mention conflicting views.

The resulting Restatements have been revised, such that many subjects are now in their third edition, and subjects have been added along the way. Each Restatement contains an index and a table of contents. Restatements are now published on the following topics: Agency, Conflict of Laws, Contracts, Foreign Relations Law of the United States, Judgments, the Law Governing Lawyers, Property, Restitution, Surety and Guaranty, Torts, Trusts, and Unfair Competition.

---

1. www.ali.org.

The Restatements have had an important influence in the development of U.S. law and are widely viewed as containing the considered opinion of some of the best legal scholars in the field. Restatements thus are an important secondary authority, and are often cited in court opinions as to which there is no controlling authority.

4.   Model and uniform laws

a.   Uniform laws

As interstate travel and commerce expanded in the United States, there became a need for greater uniformity of law on particular subjects. The National Conference of Commissioners on Uniform State Laws was developed in 1892 in response to this need with a stated goal of «[researching, drafting and promoting] enactment of uniform state laws in areas where uniformity is desirable and practical.»[2] The Conference oversees the preparation of proposed uniform laws that the states are then encouraged to adopt.

The name «uniform laws,» however, is a bit of a misnomer because the recommendation of the Conference does not create law in any jurisdiction. Uniform laws are merely proposals to each of the country's state legislatures with the anticipation of widespread adoption.

The term «uniform laws» is also misleading because versions of uniform laws that are adopted by state legislatures are rarely if ever adopted exactly as proposed by the Commission. Thus, even when a uniform law is adopted by most or all states, there will be variations – often substantial ones – among those states.

Some uniform laws have achieved a high degree of success, and this is particularly true in the area of commercial law. The most well-known of these efforts is the Uniform Commercial Code (U.C.C.), drafted jointly by the National Conference and the American Law Institute. The U.C.C. has been substantially adopted by all 50 states, although with some substantial differences among states.

b.   Model laws

Like uniform laws, model acts are proposed laws, but the main aim of model laws is not uniformity. Instead, model laws are designed to provide «models,» or normative elements that, in the judgment of the drafters, should be incorporated into specific legislation. There is no expectation that the entire act will be uniformly adopted, although there is a hope that individual states adopt the key aspects of the model act.

---

2.   www.nccusl.org.

III. FINDING TOOLS

There is an impressive array of tools designed to make legal research systematic and therefore manageable.

A. FINDING CASE LAW

1. Case reporters

Most decisions issued by most appellate courts are reported, although some decisions remain unreported.[3] Formal publication of cases results in the reproduction of cases in case *reporters*, which are organized to reflect the hierarchical and geographical structure of the courts. Cases within each reporter are organized in rough chronological order.

a. State court reporters

There is at least one set of case reporters for each state. Often, there are separate reporters within a state for different courts; most commonly, the state court of last resort will have its own dedicated reporter. West, a major publisher of U.S. legal materials, publishes case reporters in most states and also publishes a series of regional reporters that contain case law from a group of states in the same geographic area. A single case may thus be reported in the official state reporter (sometimes published by West), the West state reporter (if this is not the official state reporter), and the West regional reporter.

b. Federal court reporters

At the federal level, there are different reporters for cases issued at each level in the federal court hierarchy: the Supreme Court of the United States, the court of appeals, and the district court.

(1) Supreme Court reporters

Supreme Court cases are collected in the *United States Reports*, an official U.S. government publication. Because there is some delay in publication of the official reporter, two private reporters also publish U.S. Supreme Court opinions: the *Supreme Court Reporter*, published by West; and the *U.S. Supreme Court Reports, Lawyers' Edition*. Supreme Court cases are also available instantaneously on the website of the United States Supreme Court (http://www.supremecourtus.gov/) as well as numerous other free and subscription-based internet sites.

(2) Court of appeals reporter

A large percentage of federal court of appeal decisions are published. It is up to each court itself to determine whether a specific opinion will be formally

---

3.   Unreported cases are often accessible on internet databases, but in most jurisdictions, unreported decisions cannot be relied on by the parties in subsequent cases.

published. Federal court of appeals cases are published, roughly chronologically, in a West publication called *Federal Reporter*, now in its third series (each series goes through volume 999).

(3)   District court reporters

Federal district court cases are published in the *Federal Supplement*, also a West publication, now in its second series. A second reporter – the *Federal Rules Decisions* – also publishes district court decisions that deal with rulings on select federal procedural rules. A relatively small percentage of district court opinions are formally published. Recall that verdicts are rendered by juries in non-written format (the judge simply enters the verdict as the judgment of the court). As such, published trial court decisions will generally consist of court rulings on motions raising notable legal issues.

2.   Case finding tools

There are a number of finding tools that enable a researcher to readily locate cases (and other materials) on the subject of the research at hand.

a.   Digests

Digests, and particularly the American Digest system published by West, are the major tools used to locate cases on a specific topic of law. Digests are systematic indices to case law organized by topic within a specific jurisdiction.

The American Digest system is an outline of all of U.S. law, with brief summaries of and citations to pertinent case law. The West Digest system is organized much like the reporter system: there is a digest system for each state and for each of the regions represented by the regional reporters. There is also a series of federal digests (combining all reported federal case law) and one digest specific to the United States Supreme Court.

The West digest system uses a key number system to organize different areas of the law. Topics are organized in alphabetical order. Each broad topic –say «Contracts»– will be divided into many issues –«Formation of a Contract,» for instance– which in turn will be divided into numerous sub-issues – for example, «Requisites and Validity,» which in turn will be sub-divided further. Each of the issues and sub-issues will be identified by one or a range of West «key numbers,» which are specific identifiers for that specific matter. Key numbers and topics will also be found in cases reported in West reporters, making it possible to use a known case to return to the digest to find cases dealing with a similar legal question. What's more, the West topic and key number system is uniform across all digests, facilitating research on the same issue in a number of different jurisdictions.

Digests are divided into series, each covering different time periods. In addition to the topic and key number system, West digests can be accessed by case name, a general index, or the table of contents. Digests are updated with supplements and pocket parts.

b. Legal Encyclopedias/Treatises/American Law Reports

Legal encyclopedias, treatises, and the *American Law Reports*, discussed above, can also be used as case finding tools. If these resources lead you to a useful case but one that is not from your jurisdiction, the digest system can help you locate similar cases in your jurisdiction.

c. Citator Systems

Citator systems provide another useful mechanism for locating cases relevant to a specific research question. Citators provide citations to sources that have cited to the source in question. For example, if one were to run a case citation through a citator, the result would list every case and law review article that cited the case in question.

Citators have another essential function: They provide subsequent history to a case so that the researcher can ascertain whether the case is still valid law or whether it has been overruled, modified, or reversed on appeal.

There are two primary citator systems, both of which are available on on-line legal research programs. Westlaw (Thompson/West)) offers Key Cite, and Lexis/Nexis offers Shepard's Citators.

B. FINDING STATUTES

1. Sources of codified law

The United States Code (U.S.C.) is a systematic compilation of effective federal laws. The U.S.C. is issued in full every six years and updated as necessary. The U.S.C. is divided into fifty (50) titles, each of which is divided into sequentially numbered sections. New federal laws are incorporated into the existing code.

The first five titles of the U.S.C. deal with General Provisions (Title I), The Congress (Title II), The President (Title III), The Flag and Seal, the Seat of Government, and the States (Title IV), and Government Organization and Employees (Title V). The remaining titles (including the Judiciary and Judicial Procedure (Title 28)) are organized alphabetically by subject.

Federal legislation can also be found in Statutes at Large, which are published volumes of legislation in order of enactment.

State legislation is generally available in similar formats.

2. Annotated codes

The United States Code is also commercially prepared in annotated form, and these annotated versions of the Code are far preferable than the official version for research purposes. These publications are the United States Code Annotated (U.S.C.A.) (Thompson/West) and the United States Code Service (U.S.C.S.) (Lexis/Nexis). These services contain the text of the official code organized in the same way as the United States Code (*i.e.*, by title and section number). In addition, the U.S.C.A. and U.S.C.S. also include references to case law in which specific statutory provisions have been interpreted and applied. Both the U.S.C.S. and the U.S.C.A. contain indices by specific topic within each legislative section to facilitate locating relevant cases. Citations to other resources such as law review articles, digests, legal encyclopedias, are also included. The U.S.C.S. also provides citations to relevant provisions of the Code of Federal Regulations (see below). The U.S.C.A. and the U.S.C.S. also provide annotations for each provision of the U.S. Constitution, including the amendments.

Most state legislation has similarly annotated codes.

C.   FINDING AGENCY AND OTHER EXECUTIVE MATERIALS

At the U.S. federal level, there are several types of administrative materials. First, there are executive orders, which are presidential directives to other executive government officials. Second, there are agency issuances, usually in the form of regulations or orders in specific adjudicative events. Both regulations of general applicability and orders must be issued in a manner consistent with the agency's enabling laws, with the Administrative Procedure Act, and with agency procedures.

The issuance of regulations must also follow certain notice and comment procedures as specified in the Federal Register Act. The Federal Register is a daily publication of all notices and issuances of the federal government. Rules and regulations of general applicability are codified in the Code of Federal Regulations (C.F.R.). The Code of Federal Regulation, like the United States Code, is organized into fifty (50) titles, but caution is needed, as the title numbers of the Code of Federal Regulations do not correspond perfectly to those of the United States Code.

IV.   CITATION CONVENTION

The citation for a particular source of law is the unique address (or addresses) of the source in question. The citation serves two important functions: First, it enables a reader to locate the source referred to; and second, it provides important information about the source itself. That information, in turn, may enable the reader to ascertain, for example, the relevance and importance of a specific legal authority to the question at hand.

The Bluebook, now in its eighteenth edition, remains the leading convention for law citations in the United States, although a recent competitor published by the Association of Legal Writing Directors has been gaining ground in recent years. Both contain extensive indices to assist in locating the appropriate citation convention. The inside covers of *The Bluebook* also offer examples of how to cite the most common legal sources. Slightly different formats are used depending on whether the document is for law practice (*e.g.*, an interoffice memorandum, a court submission) or for publication (*e.g.*, a book, an article).

When preparing a legal document in the United States, one of the guides to citation convention should always be consulted. Nevertheless, a few basic rules can be stated:

Cases

- Case name, italicized or underlined.
  - Names of parties, separated by a lower case «v.»
  - For natural persons, only the last name is used.
  - If there is more than one party on each side, only the first party's name is indicated.
  - There are recognized abbreviations for many designations in party names.
- Volume number; reporter name, properly abbreviated; page number at which case begins.
- Parenthetical, which should contain:
  - Year of decision.
  - Court and jurisdiction, to the extent not clear from the reporter name.
- Some examples:
  - *Grutter v. Bollinger*, 539 U.S. 306 (2003).
  - *United States v. Sterley*, 764 F. 2d 530 (8th Cir. 1985).
  - *Campbell v. Sirak*, 476 F. Supp. 21 (S.D. Ohio).
  - *Woolley v. Hoffman-LaRoche, Inc.*, 99 N.J. 284, 491 A. 2d 1257 (1985).

Short citation forms can be used for subsequent references to the same case in the same document.

- *Id.* for the same source last cited in your document (if the prior citation contained only one source).
- *Id.* at [page number] for a different page of the same source last cited in your document (if the prior citation contained only one source).
- First name of the case (italicized or underlined), followed by a comma and the volume and name of the reporter, followed by «at [page number]». Example:
  - *Grutter*, 539 U.S. at 310.

U.S. Constitution

- U.S. Const. amend. XIV.
- U.S. Const. art. I, §2, cl. 3.

Federal Statutes

- Statutory code title number.
- Abbreviated name of statutory code.
- Section number.
- Year of code, in parenthesis.
- Example:
  - 12 U.S.C. §1989 (2002).

Books

- Author, title (underlined or italicized), page (edition, if not first edition; and year in parenthesis).
- Example:
  - Toni M. Fine, *American Legal Systems: A Resource and Reference Guide* (1997).

Articles

- Author, title (underlined or italicized), volume number of journal, abbreviated name of journal and page at which article begins (year in parenthesis).
- Example:
  - Toni M. Fine, *Moratorium 2000: An International Dialogue Toward a Ban on Capital Punishment*, 30 Colum. Hum. Rts. L. Rev. 421 (1999).

V. FINDING U.S. LAW ON THE WORLD WIDE WEB

Few libraries outside of the United States will have anything approaching complete U.S. law collections. The most comprehensive sources of online U.S. legal materials are provided by fee-based services, especially Westlaw and Lexis. Fortunately, there is a wealth of material on U.S. law available on free internet sources.

The U.S. Constitution can be found on several official government locations, for example:

- http://www.house.gov/Constitution/Constitution.html
- http://www.gpoaccess.gov/constitution/

A number of other websites also provide the text of the U.S. constitution, including searchable versions, such as:

- http://www.usconstitution.net/const.html
- http://www.law.cornell.edu/constitution/constitution.overview.html
- http://www.findlaw.com/casecode/constitution/

Federal case law is also readily available on the internet. The official website of the federal courts, www.uscourts.gov, provides links to all federal courts, most of which house opinion databases. Federal case law is also available at a number of other sites, such as those listed below.

The United States Code can be searched via http://www.gpoaccess.gov/uscode/, and the Code of Federal Regulations can be searched using http://www.gpoaccess.gov/cfr/index.html.

Some excellent general websites and search engines for U.S. legal material include the following:

- www.findlaw.com
- www.lii.law.cornell.edu
- www.llrx.com
- http://jurist.law.pitt.edu
- www.hg.org
- www.abanet.org
- www.google.com

CHAPTER V

COMMON LAW DEVELOPMENT AND THE USES OF PRECEDENT

I.   COMMON LAW AND COMMON LAW DEVELOPMENT

Common law systems like that in the United States are distinct from civil law systems like those on continental Europe in that they adopt judicial decisions as a major source of law and use them as precedent – often binding precedent – in deciding future cases. Common law is law that is developed by judges rather than embodied in a fixed body of legal rules such as a code in a civil law system.

A basic feature of common law thus is the doctrine of precedent under which judges use legal principles established in earlier cases to decide new cases that have similar facts and raise similar legal issues. Judges thus often establish legal rules that have an impact that extends beyond the parties before them in that particular case. This tendency to follow earlier decided case law is called *stare decisis*, from *stare decisis et non quieta movere* (to stand by decisions and not disturb settled points). It is up to courts in subsequent cases to determine the boundaries of prior cases. Because a single decision will normally only address issues presented in that case, it will be left to a subsequent court to decide whether the scope and rationale of the earlier decision applies or should apply to the newly presented set of facts.

In cases in which there is no precedent, the court must reason from general principles, from analogy, and from what it believes to be reasonable and in the public interest.

Rules of *stare decisis* also apply in cases involving statutory or constitutional provisions. Once a court has interpreted and applied a constitutional or statutory provision, courts in subsequent cases look to prededent in interpreting those and related provisions.

Precedent may be «persuasive» or it may be «binding.» Binding authority, sometimes called «mandatory» or «controlling» authority, as its name suggests, is binding in a subsequent case. Binding decisions include decisions of higher courts in the same jurisdiction and, sometimes, decisions of the same court. For instance, decisions of the Supreme Court of the United States are controlling on all other courts. Decisions of a federal court of appeals are binding on all courts within that circuit – all district courts that fall within the geographic reach of the circuit, as well as the court of appeals itself.[1] Decisions of a district court, however, bind only the parties before the court in that case and do not control subsequent cases.

In the absence of mandatory authority, it is consistent with good judicial practice for a court to consider «persuasive» authority. Persuasive authority is not binding on a subsequent court but it may help a judge in the decision-making process by giving insight into how others have analyzed similar legal issues in factually analogous cases. Persuasive authority includes decisions of courts of other jurisdictions and – if not binding – decisions of coordinate courts of the same jurisdiction. For example, suppose that there is no mandatory precedent applicable to a case before a federal district court judge, *i.e.*, there is no Supreme Court precedent and no court of appeals precedent from within that circuit. The district court judge would nevertheless consider the rulings of other courts on the issue before her – district court judges within and outside of that district, and courts of appeals in other circuits, for example. The judge may adopt an approach taken in one of those cases or she may choose an altogether different approach. The persuasiveness of precedent will depend on a number of factors, including the soundness of its reasoning, the number of jurisdictions reaching the same result, the prominence of the court that decided it, and the judge who authored the opinion.

In order for precedent to be binding or even persuasive, the precedent must be *relevant* – that is, it must raise similar facts and legal issues. If a court can distinguish the facts or the legal issue presented in a case from those that formed the basis for precedent, then the court may deviate from the precedent. Indeed, one of the essential skills for lawyers working in the U.S. legal system is the ability to distinguish precedent (when the lawyer does not want the earlier decided case(s) to apply) and to analogize to precedent (when the lawyer does want the earlier decided case(s) to apply).

Also fundamental to the application of *stare decisis* is the distinction between the holding of a case and *dictum*. As discussed in greater detail below, *dicta* are statements made by a court that go beyond the legal issues or the facts presented by the case before it. The refusal to grant *stare decisis* effect to *dictum* stems from the common law's commitment to the adversarial process and the resultant belief that judges have competence to decide only those matters that are necessary for a disposition of the case before them.[2] As to those matters, which presumably have been thoroughly argued by the parties,

---

1. A specific federal court of appeals is bound by its own decisions unless overruled or reversed by the U.S. Supreme Court or by the court of appeals itself in an *en banc* ruling. Of course, subsequent panels of the court of appeals, as well as district courts within that circuit, are free to distinguish the facts presented by a subsequent case to reach a different result.
2. Indeed, this is implicit in the «case» or «controversy» requirement of Article III of the Constitution.

judges' decisions are to be treated as binding precedent. The rationale for the non-binding nature of dictum as explained by the Supreme Court is quite compelling: «The question actually before the court is investigated with care and considered in its full extent. Other principles which may serve to illustrate it, are considered in their relation to the case decided, but their possible bearing on all other cases is seldom completely investigated.»[3] *Dictum* nevertheless is worthy of respect; it may be followed by the same court in later cases and a lower court may be persuaded to follow its reasoning. But at least in principle, it is not binding on any court.

The non-binding nature of dictum presents yet another opportunity for lawyers to argue that certain statements in an earlier decided case are not binding because they should be characterized as *dicta* – and an opportunity for opposing counsel to argue that such a statement was in fact part of the earlier court's ruling and thus controlling. Ultimately, it will be up to the judge in the subsequent case to decide whether statements made in an earlier case should be treated as part of the holding or as non-binding dic*tum.*

II. WORKING WITH CASE LAW

A. ANATOMY OF A CASE

Although different aspects of particular cases will be important, a reader should be careful to note the following elements of a judicial opinion:

1. Basic information about the case.
2. Material facts.
3. Procedural history/procedural posture.
4. Legal issue(s).
5. Holding.
6. Rationale.

Each of these elements is discussed below.

1. Basic information about the case.

The jurisdiction and hierarchy of the court that issued the opinion and the date of the opinion are relevant to the precedential value of the case and the application of *stare decisis* principles.

2. Material facts.

Material facts are those that are important to the case and the court's decision. The facts that underlie a court's decision are of crucial importance to the application of that case to future cases.

---

3. *Cohens Virginia*, 19 U.S. (6 Wheat.) 264, 399 (1821).

When dealing with precedent, lawyers often *analogize* to or *distinguish* the facts of their client's case from the material facts of earlier cases. Thus, an attorney who wants precedent to apply to the present case will attempt to show that the material facts presented are analogous to the material facts in the earlier-decided cases, while an attorney who does not want the earlier-decided case(s) to apply will argue that the material facts in the precedent substantially differ from the current facts so that a different result should be reached.

3.   Procedural history/procedural posture.

The procedural history of a case refers to the procedures thus far that brought the case to where it is now. What has happened since the litigation started? Readers will also want to note the procedural titles of the party (*e.g.*, plaintiff, appellant). The procedural posture refers to the procedural status of the case at the time the court decides a case. Was it on an evidentiary issue before trial? Was it on a motion for summary judgment? Was it on appeal? The procedural history and procedural posture of the case will help define the scope of the court's decision and its applicability to future cases.

4.   Legal issue(s).

The legal issue or issues are the legal question or questions presented to the court for resolution. The legal issue or issues thus help to define the holding of the case. The legal issue may be stated explicitly by the court («The issue before this Court is whether...») or may be more implicit and the reader is left to identify the legal question or questions from the context, including the court's holding.

5.   Holding.

The holding of a case is the resolution of the legal issue(s) presented. The holding of a case must be determined from an analysis of the material facts, from the court's decision, and from the reasoning of the opinion. Sometimes the procedural posture of a case will be relevant to defining the scope of the holding. However, it is often difficult to know how broadly or how narrowly the court's holding should be read. One must also look beyond a single opinion to see how the opinion is read against the background of other related decisions and general principles. The precise scope of the holding may not be clear until it has been interpreted and applied in subsequent cases.

6.   Rationale.

The rationale is the court's explanation for its holding as to each issue. Why did the court reach the conclusion it did? Was it based on a statute? Did the court consider binding or persuasive court precedent? What were the policy implications behind the court's decision?

* * * *

Case reading should always be critical, which is to say that the reader should engage in a constant process of evaluation and analysis. The thoughts and questions that emerge in the mind of the reader are among the most important aspects of the case reading process. The most useful way to read a case is to question different aspects of the court's opinion – do you disagree with certain portions of the court's rationale? What about any policy concerns underlying the court's decision? Does this case reach a conclusion that differs from other cases on the same issue? If so, can you explain this? For instance, are the cases from different jurisdictions? Do the material facts or the procedural posture differ significantly? Are the cases separated by many years, thus reflecting changes in law or policy over time? Even if the cases are not inconsistent, does one case broaden or narrow or simply explain an earlier case? Does it carve out an exception to a more general rule established in earlier cases? Does it create a new general rule? Often these questions will form the basis for the most comprehensive and useful legal analysis.

B. BRIEFING A CASE

A case brief is an organized summary of the important elements of a case. A case brief is used exclusively by the person who prepared the brief, and each person, over time, develops his or her own style in preparing a case brief. A case brief should be prepared in the reader's own words (and not simply copied from the case), and it should be concise (usually no longer than one page) and easy to read (you can use bullet points and phrases rather than complete sentences). Most people use abbreviations for common words and phrases («P» or «π» for plaintiff; «D» or «Δ» for defendant).

Most case briefs include the following elements:

1. Basic Information about the Case

   - Party names and their role in the litigation;
   - Court issuing opinion;
   - Date (year) of opinion.

2. Material Facts

   - Facts that gave rise to the litigation – the «story»;
   - Facts that the court relied on in reaching its decision.

3. Procedural History/Procedural Posture

   - What happened in earlier proceedings involving this litigation;
   - How did the parties get to where the case is now (*e.g.*, appeal, motion for summary judgment)?
   - Include lower courts' disposition of the case.

4. Legal Issue(s)

    - Legal question(s) presented to the court for resolution;

    - Incorporate key facts;

    - Number each issue separately if there are multiple legal issues.

5. Holding

    - Resolution of the legal issue(s) presented;

    - Holding can be stated narrowly or more broadly. The scope of the holding of a case often is not known until subsequent cases interpret and apply the earlier case;

    - The holding will reflect a *rule*, which is a general principle to be applied in future cases.

6. Rationale

    - Explanation of court's holding as to each issue;

    - What the court said in explaining each of its holdings;

    - How and why did the court reach the decision it did?

7. Other Opinions

    - Appellate court cases are decided by a panel of judges, so for any one case there may be opinions other than the majority opinion;

    - A dissenting opinion disagrees with the majority decision and states the reasons for that disagreement. A dissenting opinion is not part of the opinion of the court, of course, and thus does not have precedential value. But the dissenting opinion may one day represent the majority opinion and may also present the losing party with a strong basis upon which to seek an appeal, if one is available;

    - A concurring opinion agrees with the holding of the majority but for different or additional reasons.

8. Comments

    - The reader's own observations about the case.

    - Should include the reader's understanding of how the case relates to other cases on related issues.

C. SYNTHESIZING CASE LAW

Once individual cases (or other sources of law) on a particular matter are identified, read, and analyzed, there is a need to *synthesize* the various sources so as to get an understanding of that particular issue. Thus, cases and other relevant legal sources must be thought of together as an integrated body of law, an endeavor that is ultimately far more important than the understanding of any individual case. Synthesis of a number of cases reflects the development and elaboration of a rule and its broadening or narrowing to meet changing conditions and to take account of the great variety of situations that may arise.

The need to synthesize case law and other relevant sources of law will arise most commonly in the context of preparation of an interoffice memorandum. An interoffice memorandum is a predictive document that will be written for a supervising attorney and/or the client, and that sets out an objective analysis of how a problem would be resolved under the applicable law. Although such memoranda vary somewhat in format from office to office, a template of a traditional interoffice memorandum is set forth in Appendix III.

III. RULES OF *STARE DECISIS*

A. GENERAL REMARKS

Stare decisis rules and the binding nature of precedent are fundamental –indeed defining– concepts in the United States legal system. *Stare decisis* is a Latin term that technically means «let it stand»; the «it» refers to precedent, or earlier decided cases. *Stare decisis* thus is the tendency of a court to follow the rulings of earlier courts on similar legal issues when presented with similar material facts. In this way, the body of earlier decided cases forms a body of precedent that binds courts in subsequent decisions. Courts tend to follow the rulings of earlier decided cases even if they would not reach the same result were it a case of first impression.

The doctrine of *stare decisis* is firmly established in the U.S., but it is a complex phenomenon, better thought of as an art rather than a science. How *stare decisis* is applied in a particular case is largely a product of judicial discretion. In some respects, the system of *stare decisis* restricts judges. To be sure, the principle of *stare decisis* does restrain judicial discretion in the sense that a court must follow principles and rules established in earlier cases. On the other hand, a system of binding precedent leaves judges with enormous discretion. For example, judges have descretion in interpreting and determining the scope of the holdings in earlier cases – all of which is relevant to the application of *stare decisis* principles. A system of *stare decisis* also gives appellate judges a large degree of power, since appellate cases can and often do bind courts in later cases.

B.   RATIONALE FOR *STARE DECISIS*

There have been many explanations for the use of precedent, including: (1) predictability; (2) fairness; (3) judicial efficiency; (4) integrity of the judicial system; and (5) conscientious judicial decision making.

1. Predictability

The use of precedent promotes predictability in the law and stability in commercial and other relationships. *Stare decisis* principles also promote stability and consistency in the development of legal principles, which in turn can lead to enhanced economic stability and growth.

2. Fairness

One of the underlying premises of the doctrine of *stare decisis* is the fundamental fairness that results when similar cases are decided in a similar way. This principle is essential to the U.S. system of justice and to basic precepts of U.S. due process. In short, a system of precedent gives the appearance of justice and the avoidance of arbitrary decision-making, as it provides a seeming neutral authority on which judicial decision-making proceeds.

3. Judicial efficiency

The use of judicial precedent as a guiding force in the legal system can promise enormous efficiencies. *Stare decisis* means that courts do not need to consider anew every legal principle that comes before them, but can turn to earlier decided cases involving the same legal issue for guidance. Importantly, once the rule of *stare decisis* becomes a guiding principle, parties whose positions are not supported by legal precedents will be discouraged, and hopefully deterred, from bringing frivolous cases and baseless appeals on well-settled points of law. For these reasons, a system of binding precedents is thought to have the effect of inducing settlements of disputes and enhancing judicial efficiency.

4. Integrity of the judicial system

It has been the U.S. experience that the use of precedent can enhance the integrity of the judicial system and judicial processes. When citizens and entities operating within a state see that courts treat similarly-situated parties in a similar way, a level of trust develops in that system that might otherwise not be present. A legal system based on precedent also tends to impress the citizenry with a sense of stability and confidence in the legal regime. If legal rules are constantly reformulated and applied inconsistently, the system gives the appearance of instability, flux, and arbitrariness. The application of reasoned principles across the board instead inspires confidence in the rule of law and the institutions that support and promote it.

5. Conscientious judicial decision making

Because the doctrine of *stare decisis* means that today's judicial decisions will be tomorrow's precedent, judges operating under a system of binding precedent have an even greater incentive to take the utmost care in formulating their opinions and in providing an adequate rationale for their decisions.

C. OPERATION OF *STARE DECISIS* PRINCIPLES

As indicated earlier, *stare decisis* is more of an art than a science. Nevertheless, there are several factors that will always be relevant in considering whether precedent is binding. This of course is the critical question in any *stare decisis* analysis: Which earlier decided case or cases, if any, will a court be required to follow? Those decisions that a court is required to follow are said to be *binding* or *mandatory* or *controlling* authority. In the absence of such authority, a U.S. court normally should consider other, non-binding or merely *persuasive*, authority. Factors that bear on whether precedent is binding include the following:

1. The similarity of the legal issue(s) presented;

2. The relationship between the court that decided the earlier case and the court now confronted with a similar issue;

3. The similarity of the facts presented; and

4. Whether the legal principle for which the earlier case is cited as precedent was *dictum* as opposed to part of the court's *holding*.

1. The legal issue presented

A threshold question that must be considered in any *stare decisis* analysis is whether the same or a similar legal issue was presented in the earlier decided case(s) and in the case currently before the court. Naturally, if the legal issue is not the same or similar, then the entire principle of *stare decisis* becomes irrelevant.

2. Relationship between the courts

Precedent is binding on a subsequent court only if it was issued by a court whose decisions are controlling – based on considerations of hierarchy and jurisdiction – on the court later called upon to resolve a similar case.

Set forth below is a description of how this works in the U.S. federal court system with regard to federal issues. These rules do not reflect the only way that a system of binding precedent could be established. The rules that are applied in the U.S. federal courts are the product of certain policy decisions. Certainly, other policy choices could have been made; indeed rules about the binding nature of precedent do vary among the federal system and the various state judicial systems.

a. Rulings of the United States Supreme Court

Rulings of the United States Supreme Court are binding, or have authoritative impact, on all federal courts. This reflects the singular nature of the United States Supreme Court as the ultimate judicial authority in the U.S. on matters of federal law.

b. Rulings of the United States courts of appeals

Rulings of a federal court of appeals are binding within that circuit. This means that a ruling of a court of appeals will be binding on subsequent panels of that same court and on all of the district courts located within that circuit. So, for example, in the absence of a contrary Supreme Court ruling, a decision of the United States Court of Appeals for the Second Circuit will be binding on the Court of Appeals for the Second Circuit itself and on all of the federal district courts within that circuit – in this example, all of the federal district courts in New York, Connecticut, and Vermont. What this means as a practical matter is that the first panel of any court of appeals to decide an issue of federal law will bind the entire circuit, absent Supreme Court intervention. Absent action by the Supreme Court, the court of appeals would have to make an *en banc* ruling to modify the circuit rule on that legal question. Because of its unwieldy and time-consuming nature, *en banc* review is rarely granted.

But the rulings of one United States court of appeals do not bind other courts of appeals and do not even bind district courts in other circuits. This leads to the somewhat anomalous result that federal law can be interpreted and applied in different ways in different parts of the country. As a policy choice, however, it is considered to be desirable to have different rules in different circuits to allow for «percolation» and experimentation with different approaches before the issue reaches the Supreme Court for resolution on a nationwide basis. In fact, a «split of authority» among or between circuits is often considered to be a compelling reason in support of a motion for a *writ of certiorari* to the Supreme Court.

c. Rulings of the United States district courts

A ruling of a U.S. district court is binding only on the parties before the court in that case; it is not binding on any other court, or even within that same court. A district court of course is supposed to consult decisions from its own court and other courts in the absence of controlling authority. But in the absence of mandatory authority, district courts can strike out on their own and reach a holding contrary to other district courts that have decided the same legal question. And they very often do.

3. Facts

The doctrine of *stare decisis* is based on the fundamental and underlying similarity among cases and the proposition that *like* cases should be decided in *like* fashion. Because U.S. courts are required by both constitutional and prudential concerns to base their rulings on the specific facts presented by the parties before them, court decisions do not endeavor to construct a rule that could be said to apply to all facts that might arise in connection with a given legal issue (even if this were theoretically possible). And because facts arising in different cases are rarely if ever precisely the same as the facts of a prior case involving other parties, courts must undertake to determine which facts were material or relevant to the outcome in the earlier decided cases. Courts thus retain considerable discretion in determining the scope of earlier decided cases, and the breadth or narrowness with which the earlier opinion will be read. Will it be interpreted more broadly, to a set of facts well beyond those presented in the earlier case(s)? Or will the court read the precedent more narrowly to apply only to the set of facts presented in the earlier case? Or did the facts of the case fall somewhere in between in a way that allows the court to exercise its discretion in reaching the decision that it wants to make? Indeed, lawyers in the U.S. expend substantial energies trying to distinguish the facts of precedent that they hope the court will not apply and analogizing, the facts of their case to the facts of helpful precedent, urging the court to apply such precedent to the facts at hand.

4. Holding *versus* dictum

U.S. courts generally limit their decisions to the facts presented by a particular case. *Dicta* are judicial pronouncements that go beyond the facts or legal issues brought to the court by the parties. One court has referred to dicta as constituting no more than «stray observations.» *Dicta* are not to be regarded as part of the court's holding, under the theory that such issues may not have been subject to the court's full consideration or adversarial argumentation by the parties. *Dicta* is not part of the court's holding and technically is not deserving of *stare decisis* or precedential effect.

Nevertheless, it is not always easy to determine what is *dictum* and what is instead part of the court's holding or rationale. Parties often make disparate arguments about what constitutes *dictum* and what constitutes part of the court's holding or rationale and thus entitled to *stare decisis* effect. Moreover, even when court statements may be technically viewed as *dicta*, a subsequent court may give them binding effect if they were well considered, as opposed to being merely a «stray observation» by the earlier court.

* * * *

It bears noting at this juncture that the *stare decisis* effect of a case is strongest where numerous precedents stand for the same principle of law.[4] Although a rule of law announced or applied only in a single precedent falls within the scope of the policy of *stare decisis*, its *stare decisis* effect is weaker. This makes sense from a theoretical as well as a practical perspective: A well-established legal rule that will have been applied in numerous factual scenarios will mean that the operative facts will be more difficult to distinguish; a rule of law more recently announced and applied to only one or a few factual variations can more easily be distinguished by courts in subsequent cases.

D. OVERRULING PRECEDENT

Stare decisis is best thought of as a *tendency* to follow similar earlier decided cases – and not an inflexible rule. While lower courts are cabined by applicable precedent issued by courts with authority to bind those lower courts, courts may overrule their own precedent. The Supreme Court stated as follows:

> The doctrine of *stare decisis* is of fundamental importance to the rule of law, [but] our precedents are not sacrosanct. We have overruled prior decisions where the necessity and propriety of doing so has been established.[5]

It is important to keep in mind that courts are reluctant to overrule themselves for the same reasons that make the doctrine of *stare decisis* so appealing in the first place – namely efficiency, even-handedness, and predictability. Consistent with this judicial aversion to overruling precedent, a court will prefer to distinguish precedent on the facts rather than overruling it when applying the precedent would work an injustice or otherwise not be desirable. It is far more common to see courts distinguishing – and thus refusing to apply – precedent on the facts than to see an explicit overruling of precedents. At times, a court will implicitly overrule earlier decisions, and it may require careful reading and analysis to determine that a court in fact has overruled precedent. Acts of overruling have even been identified in footnotes of opinions, although thankfully this is rare.

Still, courts do from time to time explicitly overrule earlier decisions, and *stare decisis* remains a principle, not an immutable rule. The U.S. Supreme Court can (and has) overruled its prior decisions. Federal courts of appeals can also overrule their own decisions, but only by *en banc* review.

When will the Supreme Court overrule its own precedent?

First, the Court will be more likely to overrule itself on a question of constitutional law than on an issue of statutory law. Why? Because Congress

---

4. The term «super precedent» has taken on some currency as a term to describe precedent that has been reaffirmed a number of times.
5. *Ring v. Arizona*, 536 U.S. 584, 587 (2002) (internal quotations and citations omitted).

is considered to have «acquiesced» in the Court's interpretation of a statute if Congress does not take action to amend the statute in response to a Court holding respecting that statute. Because Congress has the power to prospectively «undo» the Supreme Court's interpretation of a federal law, failure to do so is considered to signal legislative assent to the Court's interpretation. Judicial action that would have the effect of overruling the earlier decision would thus be inconsistent with the spirit of the doctrine of separation of powers.

But on questions of constitutional law, congressional action to undo a Court decision is not possible. Because the procedure for amending the U.S. Constitution is so burdensome, and has been exercised so infrequently, the Court itself must correct judicial errors in interpretation or application of constitutional rights. And this it has done when necessary.

Second, the Supreme Court has generally insisted on some special prudential or pragmatic considerations for overruling its own precedent, and has indicated that the following factors will be considered:

(1)   Whether the rule has proven to be unworkable in practice;

(2)   Whether the rule is subject to a kind of reliance that would lend special hardship and inequity if it were overruled;

(3)   Whether related legal principles have so far developed as to have left the old rule no more than «a remnant of an abandoned doctrine»; and

(4)   Whether facts have so changed, or come to be seen so differently, as to have robbed the old rule of significant application or justification.[6]

---

6.   *Planned Parenthood of Southeastern, Pa. v. Casey*, 505 U.S. 833, 854 (1992).

CHAPTER VI

LITIGATION AND OTHER DISPUTE RESOLUTION PROCESSES IN THE UNITED STATES

I. INTRODUCTION

The United States is a highly litigious society, yet litigation is not the only method by which the many legal disputes that arise are resolved. In addition to litigation, there are several alternative mechanisms of dispute resolution that are commonly employed in the United States. In addition, a very high percentage of both civil and criminal disputes that arise in the United States each year are resolved by agreement between the parties.

This chapter discusses dispute resolution processes in the United States – litigation and alternatives to litigation in the civil and criminal contexts, including the appellate process. The importance of settlement to the U.S. legal system is also explored. The specifics discussed in this chapter relate to the rules applied in the federal system; although each of the states employs procedures that differ from the federal system, they are similar in most fundamental respects.

II. SOME NOTES ABOUT SETTLEMENT AND PLEA BARGAINS

By far, the vast majority of disputes are resolved by agreement between or among the parties. It has been estimated that more than 90 percent of civil disputes are resolved by settlement. A similar percentage of criminal cases are resolved by plea-bargaining arrangements. Indeed, it would be difficult if not impossible for the U.S. judicial system to function if a large percentage of disputes were not resolved in advance of trial.

Settlement can occur at any stage in a dispute – from before a complaint is formally lodged in court until well into trial. Early settlement, of course, is most efficient for the legal system and for the parties. Most settlement occurs after at least some factual investigation has been conducted. As discussed below, one of the benefits of the U.S. model of pre-trial factual discovery is that it encourages wise and efficient settlements. Trial court judges often take an active role in helping the parties to explore whether settlement may be achieved.

III.   ALTERNATIVE DISPUTE RESOLUTION

A.   INTRODUCTION TO ALTERNATIVE DISPUTE RESOLUTION

Alternative Dispute Resolution (ADR) refers to the range of procedures that provide «alternatives» to court-focused dispute resolution. These mechanisms offer a number of benefits to the system and to the parties, and in recent years have become increasingly common. ADR mechanisms include mediation and arbitration, although there are a wide range of hybrid and other approaches that fall within the rubric of ADR.

B.   MEDIATION

Mediation is a non-binding process in which an impartial third person facilitates negotiations between the parties to help them to reach a settlement. Some courts now have mandatory mediation requirements under which the attorneys, and often the parties themselves, are required to appear before a court-appointed mediator to try to settle the dispute. In federal court, magistrate judges often act as mediators. In addition to court-annexed mediation, there are a number of private mediation services that the parties can employ to assist them in settling their disputes. Mediation is particularly beneficial for parties who want to resolve their disputes privately and quickly and at substantially less cost than other mechanisms, and is especially advisable in family and other matters involving personal relationships. In the end, the success of mediation depends on the parties. Although mediation often results in a settlement, mediation efforts can result in little or no progress being made toward the resolution of the dispute.

C.   ARBITRATION

Like litigation, arbitration is an adjudicative process, but differs fundamentally from litigation in that it is private, not public. In arbitration, an arbitrator or a panel of third party neutrals listens to presentations made by each party. Applying relevant legal standards, the arbitrator or panel issues a decision on the merits of the case.

Arbitration will be employed when the parties have agreed to use arbitration as a dispute resolution process. Such an agreement can be reached before the dispute arises or after a dispute between the parties has already emerged. The following is an example of a common arbitration provision found in commercial agreements in the U.S.:

> Any controversy or claim arising out of or relating to this contract, or any breach thereof, shall be settled by binding arbitration in accordance with the Commercial Arbitration Rules of the American Arbitration Association, and judgment on the award may be entered in any court having jurisdiction thereof.

The parties of course are not required to agree that arbitration be in accordance with the rules of the American Arbitration Association or any other organization. If such rules are not referenced, then the agreement should detail the rules governing the arbitral proceedings, such as the number of arbitrators, how the arbitrators will be selected and what their qualifications will be, what law will apply, where the arbitration will take place, and what powers the arbitrators will have. Other procedures, such as the extent of and procedures for discovery, can either be agreed by the parties or left to the arbitrators. All in all, the procedures in arbitration tend to be more flexible than procedures applied in courts of law, where judges are bound by the relevant procedural and evidentiary rules.

Unless specified as non-binding, agreements to arbitrate are treated as binding, and there is very limited right of appeal from arbitral awards. The judicial policy of respecting arbitral decisions is quite robust, and a decision to settle a dispute via binding arbitration thus serves as a waiver of the right to litigate in court. Under the Federal Arbitration Act (1925), an arbitral award may be challenged in court on only very limited grounds, such as that the award was procured by corruption, fraud, or undue means; that one or more arbitrators was not impartial or was corrupt; that the arbitrators were guilty of gross misconduct; or that the arbitrators exceeded their powers. The general rule is that an arbitral award will not be set aside even if the arbitrator made a mistake of law or fact.

D.   BENEFITS OF ADR MECHANISMS

Alternatives to litigation have been touted for the many benefits that they offer over litigation. First, they save time and money. Because alternatives to litigation are often less formal than litigation, and because they proceed without a jury, such procedures often can be completed more quickly and thus more cheaply.

Arbitration also allows the parties a measure of control over the dispute resolution process itself. Litigation procedures, as will be discussed in more detail below, are framed by a number of rules of procedure and evidence and controlled by judicial discretion. Arbitration, however, offers the parties the opportunity to have input into the procedural and evidentiary rules that will govern the proceedings. This not only allows for the utilization of procedures that make sense in the context of a particular dispute, but it also gives the parties themselves a sense of ownership in the process that may hasten its outcome. In mediation, the parties are in control of whether they will reach a settlement and what the contours of that settlement will be.

Depending on the nature of the proceeding and the agreement between the parties, alternatives to litigation also offer the parties privacy and confidentiality that is not available in litigation, because court records generally are open to the public. For various reasons, one or more parties to a dispute may prefer to keep the record of a dispute private, a goal that can more readily be achieved through alternative methods of dispute resolution.

Finally, alternatives to litigation can offer a more harmonious process for the resolution of disputes, which has numerous advantages, including minimal disruption to the personal and commercial relationships between the parties.

IV. CIVIL LITIGATION

A. INTRODUCTION

The rules of civil procedure in the United States are extremely complex. Civil procedure in the federal courts is governed by a number of different rules, of which the Federal Rules of Civil Procedure and the Federal Rules of Evidence are the most important. These and other federal court rules are promulgated by the U.S. Supreme Court upon the advice of the Judicial Conference of the United States, the policy-making body of the federal judiciary. The rules take effect after congressional review, and have the same force as laws passed by Congress.

The Federal Rules of Civil Procedure govern procedural issues in civil cases in the federal courts, and the Federal Rules of Evidence govern the admissibility of evidence in civil cases before the federal courts. Each district court also has its own rules of procedure that supplement the federal rules. Individual judges may also have specific rules that are applicable to parties who appear before them. The presiding judge will also issue orders in a specific case that are applicable to the parties in that case.

Each state has a set of procedural and evidentiary rules governing the conduct of matters before the courts of that state.

B. THE PLAYERS: THE ROLE OF THE PARTIES, THE ATTORNEYS, THE JUDGE, AND THE JURY

The players in civil litigation in the United States are the parties, their attorneys, the judge, and the jury. With the exception of the jury, these participants are all familiar to lawyers from other legal systems. But the roles of these players and their interrelationships are quite distinct in the U.S. legal system; and of course the jury adds yet another dynamic to the dispute resolution process in the U.S.

1. The parties and their attorneys

There are a few notable aspects of the role of the client and the attorney and of the relationship between the attorney and the client under the U.S. legal system that bear special mention here.

a. The adversarial system and the importance of the parties/attorneys

The U.S. system is an adversarial system, in which the parties and their attorneys have primary responsibility for defining the issues, for conducting pre-trial factual discovery, and for the presentation of evidence to the decision-makers at trial. The system relies on the parties (and their attorneys) because it is believed that the clash of adversaries before the court is most likely to allow the finder of fact to determine the truth and resolve the dispute at hand. As a result, under the U.S. adversarial model, lawyers acting as zealous representatives of their clients are viewed as having a profound responsibility for the outcome of a case. The lawyer, as the legal representative of the client, has an ethical obligation to present litigation and other dispute resolution options to the client, and to provide the client with guidance and information. Ultimately, decisions as to how to proceed belong to the client.

b. Contingency fees possible

Lawyers in the United States may charge their clients on the basis of a contingency arrangement. Under a contingency fee arrangement, the lawyer's fee is «contingent» on some recovery after trial or settlement. In the event of a recovery for the client, the lawyer will recover out-of-pocket expenses and will receive a percentage of the plaintiff's recovery. If the case is lost, the lawyer will get nothing. This type of fee enables impoverished plaintiffs to gain access to the courts.

Many cases brought under a contingency fee arrangement are settled. The lawyers who agree to represent clients on this basis are skilled at assessing the strengths of the case and generally select only those that appear to have merit.

The percentage of the proceeds paid to a plaintiff's lawyer varies from one U.S. jurisdiction to the next and according to the nature of the case. In personal injury cases, the most common rate is one third. Lawyers representing tort claimants against the United States are limited by statute to a fee of twenty-five percent. It is often the rule in the U.S. that a contingency fee in excess of fifty percent is unlawful. Most states do not allow contingency fee arrangements in certain types of cases, for instance family law cases or criminal defense representation.

Contingency fees are very commonly used in personal injury litigation, as well as in shareholder derivative actions, securities fraud, and antitrust litigation.

c. No attorney fee shifting

In contrast to the way that fees are recovered in most legal systems, there is a general rule of no fee-shifting in the United States, which means that each party pays its own attorney fees, regardless of who wins the litigation. While the loser does have to pay some court fees, they are usually very small, and they are not in any way tied to the size of the plaintiff's claims, as is common in some countries.

Of course there are exceptions to the general rule. Congress by statute has provided for one-way fee shifting in specific kinds of cases. Similar legislation has been enacted in many states. Under these statutory schemes, one-way fee-shifting is utilized as an incentive to plaintiffs and their attorneys to bring certain kinds of cases in which damage awards alone might not provide sufficient incentive. Courts also have inherent power to order that a losing party pay attorney fees to the winner, but this authority is rarely invoked.

2. The judge

The trial judge has a relatively neutral role in the progression of a case. The judge is not involved in defining the legal issues. The judge is also largely absent from the process of factual discovery and undertakes no independent factual investigation. The judge generally speaking does not actively participate in the presentation of evidence through the questioning of witnesses or otherwise. The judge's main roles include issuing scheduling orders for the progress of the case; encouraging the parties to engage in settlement or other dispute resolution mechanisms; making decisions about the admissibility of evidence, both before and during trial; participating in the questioning of prospective jurors and the jury selection process; keeping order in the courtroom; making important legal rulings; and instructing the jury on the legal standard(s) that they are to apply during deliberations in reaching a verdict.

Nevertheless, this is not to say that judges in the U.S. are without power; indeed, given the role of precedent and rules of *stare decisis* in the United States,[1] and especially the role of judicial review,[2] judges – especially appellate judges – have an enormously important role in specific cases before them and in the development of law in the U.S. What they may lack in terms of direct control over evidence and the progression of trials, they certainly make up for in terms of the exercise of discretionary power in cases before them and in influence over the development of the law.

3. The jury

a. Introduction to the jury system

The jury is a very important and very interesting phenomenon in U.S. law. The jury is charged with making determinations of fact in civil (and criminal) trials. This includes decisions as to liability but also the amount of damages, if any, to be paid in a civil case.

---

1. See Chapter V.
2. See Chapter III.

The right to a trial by jury in the U.S. in most civil and criminal trials is deeply rooted in our history and Constitution, and is regarded as central to American notions of fundamental due process. The Sixth Amendment requires that almost all criminal defendants have counsel, and that counsel be provided to those who cannot afford their own lawyer. The Seventh Amendment to the U.S. Constitution guarantees the right to a jury trial in most federal civil cases, other than cases brought in equity such as admiralty suits and suits for injunctive relief. A similar provision can be found in the constitutions of all fifty states.

The jury plays an enormously important role in the U.S. judicial processes. The role of the jury is to evaluate the evidence presented at trial and decide facts that are in dispute. The jury that sits as a fact finder at a trial is known as a «petit jury.» which is different from the «grand jury» that is sometimes used in criminal cases. When we speak simply of a «jury», we generally are referring to the «petit jury.» If the parties do not request a jury trial, then the judge decides both questions of law and fact in what is called a «bench trial.»

b. Advantages and drawbacks

There are certain advantages and disadvantages associated with the jury system as utilized in the U.S., as outlined below.

(1) Advantages of the jury system

Many advantages to the jury system have been identified, for example, that it (a) enhances the prospects for settlement; (b) promotes confidence in the system; and (c) allows for the active participation of the public in the administration of justice.

(a) Improved chances for settlement

The fact that jury trials are costly and time-consuming has been cited as one inducement to settlement and may well be responsible for the high number of settlements that are reached in civil and criminal cases in the U.S. Concerns about juries acting irrationally are probably greatly overstated, but the risk of an unpredictable jury is thought to serve as an incentive to settlement. As noted below, the added cost of a jury trial may also work as an inducement to settlement.

(b) Confidence in the system

The right to a jury trial in the U.S. embraces the highly democratic notion that one should be judged only by one's peers. For this reason, the jury is selected from among a cross-section of the community in which the trial is to take place. The fact that the administration of justice is undertaken largely by one's peers rather than by professional judges who may be thought to be far removed from the people imbues the system with greater credibility and bestows heightened confidence in the outcomes achieved.

(c) Public participation in the administration of justice

The jury system in the U.S. allows participation by the public in the administration of justice to an enormous extent. Francis Lieber, a highly-regarded political philosopher, perhaps said it best when he noted that the jury system «awakens confidence» in the law and the legal system. By giving the citizen «a constant and renewed share in one of the highest public affairs, it binds the citizen with increased public spirit to the government of his commonwealth».[3]

(2)   Criticisms of the jury system

The jury system has also been subject to significant criticism, including that (a) the jury system adds to the expense and delay attendant to trials; (b) the presence of the jury imparts a certain level of inflexibility to the trial procedure; and (c) juries cannot be relied upon to reach rational decisions, especially in complex or highly emotional cases.

(a)   Time and cost

The presence of a jury in a very large number of civil trials in the United States increases the time needed and the expense involved in bringing a case to trial. First, a jury must be selected for each case, a procedure that involves the parties and, usually, the judge and other judicial officers. Second, evidence to be relied on in the case will need to be introduced more slowly and more formally when the fact-finding is to be done by the jury. The presence of a jury also means that the judge must formally «charge» or instruct the jury as to the applicable law. This can be a very complex undertaking depending on the nature of the case and the legal issues involved. Finally, jury deliberations may take some time before a verdict is reached. The need for a unanimous verdict in many civil cases (depending on the jurisdiction) may result in some delay in the announcement of a verdict. There is also the possibility of a mistrial, either because of some incurable procedural error or because the jury could not agree on a verdict (known as a «hung jury»). Either way, a mistrial necessitates a new trial thereby adding expense and delay.

(b)   Rigidity of procedures

The presence of the jury means that trials in the United States take place as concentrated events. Although they may go on for some weeks or even months, the trial will convene as a continuous event from beginning to end. This contrasts sharply with the experience in other countries in which trials often occur on a more random basis on non-consecutive days over a period of months.

---

3.   Francis Lieber, *On Civil Liberty and Self Government* 235 – 37 (2d ed. 1874).

The presence of the jury also necessitates the use of somewhat rigid trial procedures. As noted above, the presence of a jury trial mandates adherence to the rules of evidence. In addition, accommodation must be made for certain discussions that need to take place between counsel and the judge outside of the presence of the jury.

(c) Irrational decision-making

Perhaps the largest criticism of the jury system is that a lay jury is ill equipped to make factual decisions in complex cases and that use of the jury often leads to irrational outcomes. Jury decisions may also be suspect when dealing with emotionally charged matters. While most scholars believe that this criticism is overstated, there are some that remain concerned that jury members are unduly influenced by passion and other factors that should not properly form the basis for their decisions.

C. AN OVERVIEW OF CIVIL LITIGATION

A civil lawsuit is brought by the plaintiff against a defendant and begins with the filing of a complaint in court. Other parties may be involved in the litigation, as well. Civil cases may be brought by or against corporations, which are treated as separate legal entities under U.S. law. The U.S. civil system strives to balance the often competing interests of efficiency and economy on the one hand and substantial justice on the other hand.

Civil litigation in the U.S. involves a continual process of narrowing down the issues that remain in dispute between the parties. In the sections that follow, note the many opportunities for the parties and the judge to limit the legal and factual issues that remain in dispute.

1. Starting the litigation: Preliminary considerations

Before filing a complaint, the plaintiff must consider where to file the complaint. There are three issues that come up in this context: Subject matter jurisdiction; personal jurisdiction over the defendant; and venue. A related consideration involves choice of law. These matters were discussed in greater detail in Chapter III.

2. The complaint

A federal civil lawsuit begins with the filing of a complaint in the office of the clerk of the district court. The Federal Rules of Civil Procedure govern the filing of the complaint and other pleadings in federal court.[4]

---

4. Pleadings are the formal documents that define the factual and legal nature of the case. In a simple case, the pleadings are limited to the complaint and the answer. Under Rule 11 of the Federal Rules of Civil Procedure, a lawyer's signature constitutes certification that the lawyer has read the pleading; that to the best of his knowledge the statements in it are factually correct and legally justifiable; and that the filing is not being made for any improper purpose, such as to harass the defendant. The court may order appropriate relief against an attorney and/or a party for violation of this rule.

The Federal Rules of Civil Procedure require only «notice pleading,» meaning that pleadings are required only to put the opposing party on «notice» of the allegations against him. The complaint itself sets forth the basic allegations that form the basis for the plaintiff's claim against the defendant. The complaint will include a statement of the basis for subject-matter jurisdiction and the court's jurisdiction over the defendant; a statement of venue; basic factual allegations that underlie the complaint; the cause(s) of action against the defendant; and the remedy that the plaintiff seeks. Each allegation of the complaint is to be set forth in a separate numbered paragraph. The plaintiff must make a written demand for a jury trial in order to preserve that right. This demand is usually made in the complaint but may be made within ten days after service of the last pleading related to the complaint.

In addition to filing the complaint in court, the plaintiff must formally serve the complaint on the defendant, although the defendant may waive formal service. A summons must also be served on the defendant to give the defendant formal notice of the lawsuit and calling upon the defendant to answer the complaint. Rule 4 of the Federal Rules of Civil Procedure provides procedures for the service of a summons and complaint. The general rule is that service must be made so as to be reasonably calculated to give the defendant actual notice of the pending lawsuit.

A note should be made about the class action device available under U.S. law. In a class action, members of a large group or «class» of individuals sue as representatives on behalf of a class of similarly-situated plaintiffs alleged to have suffered injury arising from the same wrongful acts of the defendant. Parties may bring a class action only upon a court order allowing the case to proceed on that basis. A class will be «certified» under Rule 23 of the Federal Rules of Civil Procedure only upon a finding by the court that: (a) the class is numerous; (b) there are questions of law or fact common to the class; (c) the claims or defenses of the representative parties are typical of those of the class members; and (d) the representative parties will fairly and accurately protect the interests of the class. The court must also determine that maintaining the case as a class action is preferable to separate actions by class members.

3. Defendant's Response to the Complaint

The defendant must respond to the complaint within a specified time after service or filing of the complaint. In responding to the complaint, the defendant essentially has two choices: He may file either (a) an answer, or (b) a motion to dismiss the complaint. Failure to respond to a complaint within the time frame established by the Federal Rules of Civil Procedure can result in a default judgment being entered against the defendant. A default judgment is an order granting relief to the plaintiff due to the defendant's failure to appear in court to contest the allegations against him.

a.   Answer

An answer responds to the complaint on its merits, and consists of a paragraph-by-paragraph response to each of the allegations set forth in the complaint. For each allegation in the complaint, the defendant must state that he admits, denies, or lacks sufficient information to admit or deny the allegation.

The defendant's answer must also assert any affirmative defenses he has against the plaintiff. An affirmative defense is any basis upon which the defendant would prevail even if everything the plaintiff alleges were correct. For example, an affirmative defense could be that the statute of limitations has run on the plaintiff's cause of action.

An answer may contain a counterclaim or a cross-claim.

In a *counterclaim*, the defendant sues the plaintiff in response to the original suit. The defendant who files a counterclaim is the «counterclaim plaintiff» in the case, as well as the defendant, and the plaintiff is also the «counterclaim defendant.» The counterclaim may be compulsory or permissive. A compulsory counterclaim arises out of the same transaction or occurrence as the complaint filed by the plaintiff. A compulsory counterclaim must be made by the defendant or he will be barred from raising that claim in a separate lawsuit.

A defendant in a case involving multiple defendants may also file a *cross claim* against another defendant. In a cross claim, one defendant (Defendant A) may file a cross claim against another defendant (Defendant B), alleging that any injury to the plaintiff was caused by Defendant B. Defendant B would be both a defendant and a «cross claim defendant» in the lawsuit. Defendant A would remain a defendant in the original suit and would also become a «cross claim plaintiff» against Defendant B.

b.   Motion to Dismiss

Instead of an answer, the defendant may file a motion to dismiss. Rule 12b of the Federal Rules of Civil Procedure sets forth the following bases upon which a motion to dismiss can be filed: (1) lack of jurisdiction over the subject matter; (2) lack of jurisdiction over the person; (3) improper venue; (4) insufficiency of process; (5) insufficiency of service of process; (6) failure to state a claim upon which relief can be granted; and (7) failure to join an indispensable party.

Defenses based on lack of jurisdiction over the person, improper venue, insufficiency of process, or insufficiency of service of process are waived if not raised in the defendant's first pleading to the court.

Lack of subject-matter jurisdiction can be raised at any time by any party and is one of the rare matters that a judge may raise *sua sponte* (on his or her own motion).

A motion to dismiss for failure to state a claim upon which relief can be granted deserves special mention. In this type of motion, the defendant argues that the complaint does not state a cause of action that the law recognizes, regardless of what the facts may be, and that thus there is no legal basis to support the plaintiff's claim.

I like to think of this as the «so what?» motion. Imagine for example that I am sued because I am wearing a red sweater. There may be some question as to whether the sweater is really red or whether it is pink or maroon. But the facts do not really matter – what matters is that the law does not recognize a cause of action on the basis of the color of one's sweater, whatever that color may be. Because the law does not provide a remedy for the complaint under any set of facts, there is no reason to convene a trial on the factual issues. In such a case, the judge would simply order a dismissal of the complaint.

4. Managerial judging: Scheduling and other pre-trial orders

Judges in the United States in recent years – especially at the federal level and in some states – have taken increasing responsibility for the swift handling of cases before them. Docket control, once left primarily to the parties, has now become an important area of judicial oversight.

Under the federal rules, the trial court judge is to issue a scheduling order that is to «control the subsequent course of action unless modified by a subsequent order». Fed. R. Civ. P. 16. The scheduling order is to provide dates by which additional parties may be added or «joined» in the case; the pleadings may be amended; motions may be filed; and discovery is to be completed. The scheduling order may also set dates for pre-trial conferences and trial.

Pre-trial conferences may simply be status conferences, but they may also include efforts to simplify issues by stipulating to facts, limiting the number of expert witnesses who may testify at trial, and resolve pending motions. Such conferences may also be used to encourage settlement or mediation.

5. Discovery

a. Introduction

Discovery is the process by which parties learn, or «discover,» relevant facts from their adversaries and from third persons. Pre-trial fact discovery in the Untied States is extremely expansive and a time-consuming and expensive phase of litigation that, in complex cases, can take years to complete.

The power of lawyers to conduct discovery is related to the right to a jury trial and to the adversarial tradition in the United States. Because a jury trial must be oral and continuous, the evidence to be presented to the jury for its consideration must be in the possession of the attorneys before the trial begins. And, consistent with the adversarial tradition, discovery in civil cases is conducted primarily by the parties largely without the direct participation of the court. A party may, however, request the court's intervention in certain circumstances.

Discovery enables each party's lawyer to know more precisely what evidence may be needed to refute the contentions of the opposing party. Discovery procedures in the U.S. have a number of practical effects: reducing the likelihood of unfair surprise, thereby allowing for a smoother progression of the trial; increasing the likelihood of better informed settlements because lawyers and clients can better assess the strengths and weaknesses of their opponent's case and the relative risks and benefits of proceeding to trial; and increasing the cost of litigation. Some say that expansive discovery rules have also enhanced the potential for abuse by some lawyers who use the discovery processes as a «fishing expedition» to uncover wrongdoing by others.

b.   Scope of discovery

(1)   Broad discovery permitted

The scope of discovery in the U.S. is vast. The relevant federal rule (Rule 26(b)(1)) provides as follows (subject to certain exceptions discussed below):

> Parties may obtain discovery regarding any matter, not privileged, that is relevant to the claim or defense of any party, including the existence, description, nature, custody, condition, and location of any books, documents, or other tangible things and the identity and location of persons having knowledge of any discoverable matter. For good cause, the court may order discovery of any matter relevant to the subject matter involved in the action. Relevant information need not be admissible at trial if the discovery appears reasonably calculated to lead to the discovery of admissible evidence.

(2)   Exceptions from discovery

There are a few limitations to discovery that would otherwise fall within the scope of permissible fact finding. These relate to disclosure of information that is protected by the attorney client privilege or that is subject to the work product exception.

(a)   Attorney client privilege

The attorney client privilege protects from disclosure communications that are made by a client in confidence to his or her attorney as part of the representative relationship. The privilege extends to conversations and correspondence among the client's attorneys, and also to communications between agents of a client and the client's attorney. In order to be exempt from disclosure under the attorney-client privilege, the information must not be revealed to third persons to whom the privilege does not extend. If the requirements are met, the privilege is an absolute bar against disclosure.[5] The attorney client privilege is intended to encourage full disclosure by clients to their attorneys so as to enable lawyers to be able to give informed and competent advice.

(b) Work product exception

The other significant restraint on discovery is the protection given to an opposing lawyer's «work product,» which is the work of an attorney or someone under his supervision done in preparation for or anticipation of litigation. This exception from disclosure is viewed as critical to the lawyer's ability to render professional services to a client. Were such materials readily available to opposing counsel, much of a lawyer's work would not be reduced to writing.

Unlike the attorney client privilege, the work product exception to disclosure is not absolute. Factual work product may be discoverable upon a showing of substantial need. On the other hand, «opinion» work product – that which reflects counsel's subjective impressions, thoughts, and strategies, for example – is almost always protected.

c. Discovery devices

The Federal Rules of Civil Procedure authorize numerous discovery devices: (1) Interrogatories; (2) Depositions; (3) Requests for Production of Documents and Other Things; (4) Requests to Admit; and (5) Physical and/or Mental Examination. In most cases, the parties engage in multiple forms of pretrial discovery.

(1) Interrogatories

Interrogatories are written questions submitted to a party by the party seeking discovery; they cannot be submitted to persons who are not parties to the case. Interrogatories are to be answered in writing, under oath. Interrogatories are often used in the early stages of a case to get basic information, including the identity of witnesses who may have relevant information. Interrogatories can also be very helpful in beginning to define the factual contentions of the adversary.

(2) Requests for production of documents and other things

A party may request that the opposing party make certain specified documents and other objects available for inspection and copying. The right to review an adversary's files includes the right to have access to electronic records.

---

5. There are very limited exceptions to this absolute bar, for example if an attorney knows that the client is about to commit a crime of violence that may lead to serious bodily injury or death.

Very often, especially in large cases, the party responding to the document requests will invite the opponent's lawyers to the respondent's offices to inspect and copy relevant documents. This can become an especially time-consuming and expensive process for the party requesting the discovery, as the attorneys will often have to review many boxes of documents in order to find relevant material.

Witnesses who are not parties to the lawsuit are not subject to this form of discovery. Documents in the possession of such witnesses are accessible through the subpoena process. A subpoena is a court order that requires a person to appear at a trial, hearing, or deposition for the purpose of testifying as a witness. A subpoena may direct a person to produce documents in his possession without having to testify. A subpoena *duces tecum* requires the person both to appear and to produce relevant documents.

(3)   Depositions

A deposition is a sworn statement made by a party, witness, or other person who may have information about the case. During the deposition, the attorney who requested the deposition asks questions of the deponent relating to the case. The opposing attorney is present, and the deponent may have his own attorney. Testimony is taken under oath, and an official court reporter is present to record the testimony. With increasing frequency, depositions are recorded by electronic means, including videotape. Such recordings may be used if the witness is not available to testify at trial.

Depositions are generally taken in the offices of the attorney calling the deposition. If the deponent is a party or an employee of a party, no subpoena is needed – all that is required is to give timely notice to the deponent and to the opponent's counsel of the time and place. Normally, the time is subject to negotiation between the parties.

(4)   Requests to admit

Requests to admit ask the receiving party to admit the truth of certain facts if they are true; to deny them if they are not true; or to state that the party does not have sufficient information to admit or deny the fact in question. The party refusing to admit the truth of statements proffered is at risk of paying the costs of proving any fact he unreasonably refused to admit.

(5)   Physical or mental examination

A party may be able to obtain a physical or mental examination of another party if that party's physical or mental condition is in controversy and there is good cause for the examination. This form of discovery may be invoked only against parties, not third party witnesses.

d. Discovery practice and procedure: The role of the court

As noted above, the process of discovery is party-driven. The judge does have broad authority to control discovery, a power that is evident in the court's establishment of a time frame within which discovery must be completed. Because discovery tends to be such a protracted process, courts are becoming more and more vigilant in enforcing deadlines established for the completion of discovery.

Courts may also be called upon to resolve disputes between the parties that arise during the discovery process. Courts look rather unkindly toward discovery motions and parties are well advised to make every effort to resolve discovery disputes between themselves before resorting to the court.

Disputes that may warrant the court's attention generally arise in the context of a motion for an order to compel discovery or a motion for a protective order.

(1) Motion to Compel

A motion for an order to compel discovery arises when one party believes that another party is not responding – or not responding adequately – to its discovery requests. The motion asks the court to order the recalcitrant party to respond to legitimate discovery requests lodged by the moving party. In response to such a motion, the court may issue an order to show cause, which instructs the non-moving party to «show cause» why it should not be required to respond to the discovery at issue.

(2) Motion for Protective Order

A motion for a protective order is a request by a party receiving discovery requests that the court «protect» it from abusive discovery. A party filing such a motion often claims that the opponent is on a «fishing expedition» by seeking broad discovery in the hope of finding material that may give rise to some wrongdoing. An order issued by the court in response to such a motion can establish limits on the discovery sought by the non-moving party. A protective order issued by a court can also include a limitation on who can read the information to be disclosed or an order that the information not be disclosed to third persons.

6. Summary judgment motions

Rule 56 of the Federal Rules of Civil Procedure allows any party to file a motion for summary judgment against another party.

A motion for summary judgment asks the judge to decide the case, or some portion of the case, without a jury. Such a motion may be granted when there are no material facts in dispute or when the factual evidence to support the facts asserted by the non-moving party are so insubstantial that no reasonable jury could find for that party. Accordingly, the motion can be granted only if there are no material facts in dispute or in the absence of some credible factual evidence in favor of the non-moving party. The court cannot resolve material facts legitimately in dispute and cannot make judgments about the credibility of facts reasonably in dispute at the summary judgment stage – those tasks are reserved for the finder of fact at trial.

A motion for summary judgment may be filed as to the entire case or only as to certain issues in the case. If a motion for summary judgment is granted as to the entire case, the case is over, subject to the right of the non-moving party to appeal the grant of summary judgment. If a motion for summary judgment is denied, or is granted as to only part of a case, the case proceeds to trial. Denials of summary judgment motions are not appealable.

7. Other pre-trial motions

Any number of pre-trial motions in addition to those discussed above may be made by one of the parties. The most common of such motions are motions to exclude specific evidence from the trial, often called motions *in limine*. Parties often like to resolve issues about the admissibility of evidence in advance of the trial to minimize the risk that the jury will hear evidence that may ultimately be deemed to be inadmissible. Although the judge would instruct the jury to not consider such information, it may be difficult for jurors to disregard information that they have heard, even when instructed otherwise.

8. Trial

Trials in the United States are discrete and isolated affairs. This is largely due to the presence of the jury and the need to therefore present the evidence sequentially. Also, because of the extensive system of pre-trial discovery in the U.S., the parties are able to better prepare for trial in advance, and the element of surprise at trial is thus substantially reduced.

Once a jury is chosen and sworn in, the trial begins. The trial proceeds in the following stages: Opening statements by both sides; presentation of plaintiff's evidence; presentation of defendant's evidence; closing statements; the jury charge and jury deliberations; and the entry of the jury's verdict as the court's judgment.

a. Selecting the jury

Jury service is considered to be both a right and a responsibility of citizenship. The selection of a jury involves several stages: Developing a pool of potential jurors, excluding jurors who are ineligible to serve, and then engaging in the process of *voir dire*. The process of *voir dire* is intended to ascertain if any of the prospective jurors are unfit to sit on that particular case. Through this process, the attorneys may remove potential jurors based on challenges to specific individuals.

(1)   Developing the pool

Prospective jurors may be identified from voting records, driver registration records, or other means. The jury pool should be as comprehensive as possible in its inclusion of adult citizens that reside in that community.

(2)   Automatic exclusions

Certain categories of persons are subject to automatic exclusion from jury service. Non-citizens, persons under the age of eighteen, persons who have been judged to be mentally incompetent, and persons who do not speak and understand English well enough to meaningfully participate are excluded from service. In many jurisdictions, persons convicted of a felony are subject to an automatic exclusion from jury service.

(3)   *Voir Dire*

(a)   Introduction and overview

The judge and sometimes the lawyers will question prospective jurors about potential conflicts of interest or other reasons that might suggest that a prospective juror will not decide the case impartially. This process of questioning is called «voir dire.» In federal court, the judge controls *voir dire*, although the judge will seek the input of counsel as to specific areas of inquiry that may be relevant to the case. Among other things, prospective jurors may be asked about their occupation, their familiarity with the law, their familiarity with the facts relating to the case, their acquaintance with any of the parties, witnesses, or attorneys involved in the case, and any strong feelings or experiences that could make it difficult for them to decide the case fairly and impartially.

The process of selecting a jury is considered to be an extremely important part of the trial. In fact, a cottage industry of jury consultants has emerged to assist attorneys in the selection of jurors. This is because jury selection inevitably involves sociological profiles and stereotypes that may be based on a variety of factors, including gender, age, political affiliations, family life, employment, and professional associations.

(b)   Challenges to prospective jurors

During the process of *voir dire*, the attorneys have the opportunity to prevent a prospective juror from sitting on the jury for that case through a system of *challenges* to prospective jurors. There are two types of challenges permitted: *Challenges for cause* and *peremptory challenges*.

(i)   Challenges for cause

A lawyer may challenge a prospective juror for cause if the juror's answers to questions suggest that he or she cannot decide the case impartially. If the judge agrees with the lawyer who challenges the prospective juror, the juror will be excused and will not sit on the jury for that particular case. There are no limits to the number of prospective jurors that can be challenged for cause, but judges will vary in how permissive they will be in granting such challenges.

(ii)   Peremptory challenges

An attorney has a limited right to prevent prospective jurors from sitting on a case without stating any reason. Unless the judge orders otherwise, each lawyer in a civil case in federal court is entitled to three peremptory strikes.

The purpose of peremptory challenges is to provide the parties with some protection against any arbitrary prejudices they may sense on the part of a prospective juror. This right is not unlimited, and the Supreme Court has held that the right to remove jurors may not be exercised on racial or ethnic grounds or on the basis of gender. When it appears that jurors may have been stricken for such a reason, counsel may be asked to give another justification for removing that particular juror.

* * * *

Once the attorneys have had the chance to challenge prospective jurors, the jurors for that particular case will be chosen from the prospective jurors who remain. Generally, this is done by selecting the first twelve (the number of jurors that traditionally sit, but this is not always the case) of the remaining potential jurors. The others are dismissed or sent back to be questioned to sit as jurors on other cases.

b.   Opening statements

The trial itself starts with opening statements made by the attorney for each side. Opening statements are not evidence, but give the lawyers the opportunity to summarize and explain to the jury the evidence that will be introduced over the course of the trial. The plaintiff's lawyer always makes an opening statement at the start of the trial. Counsel for the defense has the option of making an opening statement right after the plaintiff's opening statement or of waiting until the plaintiff's evidence has been presented and the defense is about to present its evidence.

c.   Introduction of evidence

The introduction of evidence into the record is the heart of any trial. Evidence includes testimony, objects, and documents. The testimony of a party's witnesses and any documents or other things introduced with their testimony becomes the party's evidence comprising its case in chief.

Oral testimony, also known as «testimonial evidence,» is the primary method for the receipt of evidence at trial. There are two types of witnesses that may be called – fact witnesses and expert witnesses. Fact witnesses are persons who have personal knowledge of facts or events related to the case. An expert witness may or may not have direct information about the case but will testify as to something within his or her recognized expertise that bears on some issue in the case. The common use of experts in trials has resulted in the emergence of experts in various fields who are willing to testify to almost any opinion. This in turn can lead to a «battle of the experts» at trial which results in added time and expense and, often, significant jury confusion.

Testimonial evidence is introduced through witness testimony. Each party calls witnesses to the stand and asks questions of each witness. Each witness takes an oath or affirmation that he or she will tell the truth. The initial questioning of a witness by an attorney is called «direct examination.» When the direct examination of a witness is concluded, counsel for any other party may ask the witness questions relating to the direct testimony of that witness. This is known as «cross examination.» Cross examination is designed to test the credibility of a witness by showing that the witness's testimony was influenced by bias on the part of the witness or was the product of a faulty memory or perception. After cross examination of a witness, the party who initially called the witness is given the opportunity to question the witness about matters that were raised for the first time on cross examination. This is called «redirect examination.»

Documentary evidence may also be received at trial. The rules of evidence require that the relevant contents be read into the trial record by a witness who can testify as to the authenticity of the document.

Once the plaintiff has presented its case in chief by having introduced all of its evidence, the defendant has the chance to call its witnesses. As with the witnesses presented by the plaintiff, the direct examination of the defendant's witnesses will be followed by cross examination and re-direct examination.

Before putting on its case in chief, the defendant may make a motion to the court that it order judgment as a matter of law pursuant to Rule 50 of the Federal Rules of Civil Procedure. In this motion, made outside of the presence of the jury, the defendant asks the judge to rule that the plaintiff has not introduced sufficient credible evidence on one or more claims to allow that claim to go to the jury. If the judge agrees, the court will enter «judgment as a matter of law» and the trial will be over as to that issue or those issues. These motions are not frequently granted.

As noted above, the Federal Rules of Evidence controls the admissibility of evidence in civil trials in federal court. These rules are quite complex, and parties often disagree about the admissibility of specific pieces of evidence. The trial judge is thus often called upon to rule on counsel's objection to the admissibility of specific evidence during the trial. The judge usually rules on such motions in open court, in the presence of the jury. Sometimes, a party may prefer to raise an evidentiary objection outside the hearing of the jury and will ask the judge to call a «side bar conference» held between the attorneys and the judge only. This takes place quietly at the judge's bench.The judge may «overrule» an objection, in which case the witness is to answer the question; or the judge may «sustain» an objection. If an objection is sustained, the witness is instructed not to answer the question. If the witness has already answered the question, the jury will be instructed that it is not to consider that answer as evidence in the case. Depending on the nature of the information revealed by the witness, this may be difficult for the jury to do. For this reason, motions *in limine* are often preferred.

d. Closing statements

After the plaintiff and the defendant have presented their cases and all cross examination has been completed, the attorneys are given another opportunity to address the jury directly in a «closing statement.» During closing statements, the lawyers summarize the evidence and attempt to persuade the jury to draw conclusions from the evidence that is favorable to their client. Like opening statements, closing statements are not evidence but help to organize and summarize the evidence for the jury.

e. Jury charge

After closing arguments, the judge instructs the jury on the principles of law that they must apply to the case. This is known as the «charge.» The judge's charge provides the applicable rules of law that the jury is to apply to the facts as the jury finds the facts to be.

Judges often ask the attorneys to submit proposed jury instructions at some point prior to the end of the trial. The parties are encouraged to work together to try to agree to a set of jury instructions to present to the judge. When the parties are unable to agree on jury instructions, the judge will have to resolve such issues. There are form books that attorneys and judges may use in preparing jury instructions.

The charge is delivered orally by the judge in open court. The length of the jury charge will depend on the complexity of the legal issues involved in the case. Once the jury has been charged, the jurors will be dismissed to begin their deliberations. Jury deliberations are private and no one other than the jurors themselves are present during the deliberations.

One crucial element that is part of any jury charge is the burden of proof, which refers to the level of certainty required for the jury to reach a verdict. The burden of proof essentially reflects a presumption in favor of one party, which needs to be overcome in order for the other party to prevail. In civil trials, the plaintiff generally carries the burden of proof, which means that the plaintiff's attorney must prove to the jury that the defendant committed the alleged wrong. The defendant is not required to prove that he or she did not commit the wrong complained of.

In most civil cases, the plaintiff must prove its case by a «preponderance of the evidence.» What this means is that the finder of fact must be convinced that the evidence presented by the plaintiff makes it *more likely than not* that the defendant committed the alleged wrong. If the plaintiff did not convince the jury, or if the jury believes that the defendant's version of events is at least as likely as the plaintiff's version, then a verdict must be returned for the defendant.

f. Jury deliberations and verdict and the issue of punitive damages

(1) Jury deliberations and verdict

As noted, after being charged by the judge, the jury will meet in secret to consider the case before it. The jury foreperson presides over the deliberations. Depending on local practice, the foreperson may be selected by the court or by the jurors.

Rule 48 of the Federal Rules of Civil Procedure requires that a jury verdict be unanimous unless the parties agree otherwise. It should be noted that something less than a unanimous verdict is acceptable in some state courts.

The jury may be asked to deliver a general verdict or a special verdict. A general verdict simply indicates the party in whose favor the jury finds and the amount of damages to be awarded, if any. A special verdict requires that the jury provide written findings relating to each issue of fact in the case.

When the jury is ready to announce its verdict, the judge will assemble the attorneys in the courtroom. The verdict will then be read by the jury foreperson, the judge, or a court bailiff. With the reading of the verdict, the jury's service is at an end.

Occasionally, the jury cannot decide on a verdict and is «deadlocked» or «hung.» If the judge decides that there is no reasonable possibility that the jury will reach agreement after further deliberations, the judge will declare a mistrial. The case then will be scheduled for another trial before a new jury.

(2) Punitive damages

One special aspect of damages under U.S. law should be noted here and that is the availability of punitive damages.

The prevailing party in civil litigation is normally entitled to compensatory damages, which are those damages that would put the injured party in the position he would have been but for the wrongdoing. Compensatory damages are intended to make the injured party whole. In accident cases, compensatory damages may be divided between special damages (which include present and future medical expenses and earnings lost as a result of the accident) and general damages (which is compensation for pain and suffering or mental anguish associated with the accident).

A plaintiff may seek punitive or exemplary damages in addition to compensatory damages. Punitive damages, as the name suggests, are intended to *punish* the wrongdoer. Rather than compensate the injured party for a loss or injury, these damages amount to a windfall for the plaintiff. Punitive damages are not awarded in the U.S. with great frequency, and large punitive damages awards are very rare. The appropriateness of punitive damages at all, or limits to such damages, is a central issue to ongoing discussions about tort reform in the U.S.

A jury may be instructed to consider punitive damages only under limited circumstances. The law varies from state to state, but most jurisdictions require that a plaintiff prove that the defendant acted with «malice» or some other heightened standard. Punitive damages are awarded most frequently in cases in which serious physical injury or death has occurred. Punitive damages are sometimes imposed by statute, such as in the case of federal antirust violations, for which treble damages are awarded.

The Supreme Court has begun to recognize constitutional restrictions on punitive damages awards. In a number of relatively recent cases, the Court has held that excessive punitive damages may result in a deprivation of due process against the wrongdoer, and that punitive damages awards must be measured in relation to: (1) the reprehensibility of the wrongdoer's conduct; (2) the size of any compensatory award; and (3) the size of the criminal fine that might be imposed on the misconduct involved.

The benefits of punitive damages that have been identified include the following: (1) Punitive damages encourage safer and more socially acceptable behavior; (2) punitive damages serve as an incentive for private parties and attorneys to pursue cases of gross misfeasance that would give rise to such damages; and (3) punitive damages serve to express strong public disapproval of the conduct at issue.

The following criticisms have been lodged against a system of punitive damages: (1) Punitive damages are so uncertain that the prospect of such awards may discourage socially useful behavior by corporate actors; (2) the costs of punitive damages are passed down to consumers through increased prices for goods and services, while the successful plaintiff recovers a windfall profit; and (3) the prospect of punitive awards may encourage the filing of groundless claims with the expectation of a quick and lucrative settlement offer by the defendant.

9. Post trial motions

Once the verdict is announced, the losing party may ask the judge to set aside the verdict on the ground that the verdict is unsupported by the evidence, or to order a new trial. Such motions are rarely successful.

10. Entry of judgment

The judgment is the final court order formally setting forth the rights and liabilities of the parties. Rule 58 of the Federal Rules of Civil Procedure requires that the verdict be entered on a form called a «judgment.» The judgment is entered in the official court record for the case.

11. Enforcement of judgment

A party who receives an award in a civil suit may apply for enforcement of the judgment immediately after the judgment is entered, although the court may order a stay of the enforcement until the appeals process is exhausted. If necessary, the prevailing party may need to seek the assistance of the court in enforcing the judgment. In such cases, the court may authorize garnishment of the defaulting party's wages or seizure of that party's real property. Enforcement of a judgment may be difficult and may frustrate the prevailing party's victory, especially if the losing party has few or no assets.

V.   CRIMINAL LITIGATION

A.   INTRODUCTION

Criminal actions are brought for violations of criminal laws. Most criminal law is governed at the state level, but there are also a number of federal criminal offenses. Persons charged with violation of a federal offense will be tried in the federal courts.

There are two classes of federal criminal laws. Felonies are crimes that are punishable by one year or more of prison and represent most of the criminal trials in federal court. Misdemeanors are less serious crimes. Federal misdemeanors are often tried before a magistrate judge.

Plea bargaining – settlements in criminal cases – is enormously important to the U.S. criminal justice system. Most persons accused a of crime plead guilty if they are permitted to plead to an offense carrying a less severe penalty than that imposed for the more serious crime with which they originally were charged. The presiding judge must decide whether to accept the plea bargain, which he or she usually does.

Federal criminal trials are governed by the U.S. Constitution, by the Federal Rules of Criminal Procedure, and by federal statutes. State rules govern state criminal trials, but many provisions of the federal constitution are also applicable.

The judicial process in a criminal case differs from a civil case in several important respects, which will be discussed below.

The principal actors are the U.S. attorney (or the district attorney in a state criminal proceeding) and the grand jury. The U.S. attorney represents the United States in most court proceedings, including criminal proceedings, at the federal level. The defense counsel of course also has an important role, as does the petit jury, which is charged with making the determination of whether the accused is guilty or not guilty.

B.   AN OVERVIEW OF CRIMINAL LITIGATION

1.   Indictment by grand jury

In federal felony cases, a grand jury must be convened pursuant to Amendment V to the U.S. Constitution. The grand jury determines, based on evidence presented by the U.S. Attorney, whether there is sufficient evidence to require a defendant to stand trial. Although the Fifth Amendment requirement of a grand jury has not been incorporated to the states, many states also require indictment by a grand jury before a criminal prosecution can proceed.

2.   Arrest interview

After a person is arrested, he is immediately interviewed by a pretrial services officer or probation officer. The pretrial services officer or probation officer also conducts an investigation into the defendant's background. This information is used to help the judge decide whether to release the defendant before trial or whether the defendant must be held in custody (or «remanded») pending trial.

3.   Probable cause hearing

The defendant next appears before a district court judge or a magistrate judge. The judge formally advises the defendant of the charges pending against him, and determines whether there is «probable cause» to believe that an offense has been committed and that the defendant committed it. If so, the defendant is offered a court-appointed attorney if he cannot afford an attorney. At this point, the judge determines whether the defendant should be held pending trial or whether he can be released, normally upon the payment of bail.

4. Arraignment

The next phase of the criminal proceeding is the arraignment, at which the defendant is asked to enter a plea to the charges brought against him. Although most criminal cases do result in a plea bargain, most defendants enter a plea of «not guilty» at the arraignment stage. If the defendant pleads «not guilty,» the judge schedules a trial. Under the Constitution and various federal and state laws, a criminal trial must be held promptly.

5. Discovery

Criminal trials include discovery but criminal discovery procedures are far more limited than in civil cases. The prosecutor at a minimum is required to hand over any information requested by the defense and any exculpatory material, whether or not specifically requested. Exculpatory material is information that the prosecutor knows of or should know of that tends to suggest the defendant's innocence.

6. Evidentiary motions

The attorneys often file motions in advance of trial that ask the court to make rulings about the admissibility of specific evidence at trial. Most commonly, a defense attorney will make a motion to suppress or exclude certain testimony or other evidence from trial. Motions to suppress may be made to exclude evidence that the defense believes was obtained by the government in violation of the defendant's constitutional rights. Motions to suppress may also be made to exclude evidence that the defense argues would have limited probative value as to the defendant's guilt but which would be highly prejudicial to the defendant at trial.

7. Trial by jury

Trial by jury is routinely available for any serious criminal charge. Article III section 2 of the Constitution provides that «[t]he Trial of All Crimes, except in Cases of Impeachment, shall be by Jury.» The Sixth Amendment provides: «In all criminal prosecutions, the accused shall enjoy the right to a speedy and public trial, by an impartial jury».

Criminal trials proceed in much the same fashion as civil trials. The prosecution has the burden of proving the defendant's guilt «beyond a reasonable doubt.» This is a much higher standard of proof than that applied in a civil trial. Under the «beyond a reasonable doubt» standard, the government must prove to the trier of fact that there is no reasonable doubt that the defendant committed the crime.

If a defendant is found by the jury to be not guilty – which means that the prosecution did not meet its burden of proof – then the defendant is released. Under principles of double jeopardy, he may not be tried again by the same government for committing the same alleged acts.

8. Punishment

In a criminal case, the jury decides the issue of guilt but the judge imposes a sentence on a defendant who is found guilty by a jury. The one exception is that in a capital case – a case in which the prosecutor seeks to impose the death penalty – the jury must make a recommendation to the judge as to whether the death penalty should be imposed.

The judge's sentence will normally not be imposed right after the trial. Instead, a date will be set for sentencing. The convicted person may be released pending sentencing or may be remanded to prison. At sentencing, the court may consider not only the trial record but any other relevant information brought to its attention by the court's probation office or the U.S. attorney. The court may also consider victim impact statements, which may be oral or written, in which the victim describes the emotional, financial, and physical effect of the crime. The convicted person normally also has an opportunity to address the court at sentencing. In federal court, judges consult the Federal Sentencing Guidelines in fashioning a criminal sentence.

VI. APPEALS AND THE APPELLATE PROCESS

In the federal court system and in all of the states, a party aggrieved by a trial court judgment is entitled as a matter of right to appeal that decision to an appellate court, with one important exception — the acquittal of a defendant in a criminal case may not be appealed. A party aggrieved by a final decision of a federal agency also has the right to have that decision reviewed in federal court, often in the court of appeals. In the federal system, an appeal from a decision of a district court will be brought in the court of appeals for the circuit in which the district court sits; statutory venue rules govern petitions for review of agency decisions. Generally, a party may not appeal until the proceedings at the trial court have been completed, although interlocutory appeals are permitted as to certain limited matters.

A litigant who files an appeal, known as «appellant» (or «petitioner» in the case of an appeal from agency action) must show that the trial court (or agency) committed legal error that affected the outcome of the case. The appellate court will make a decision based on the record of the case established by the trial court (or agency) that rendered the decision under review. The court of appeals does not receive evidence or hear witnesses. The court of appeals may review factual findings made by the trial court or agency but will overturn a decision on factual grounds only if the findings were «clearly erroneous,» a standard that is difficult to satisfy. And an appellate court will not consider issues that the appellant did not raise before the trial court and thus did not preserve for appellate review.

Procedures in the federal court of appeals are governed by the Federal Rules of Appellate Procedure, which may be supplemented by local court of appeals rules. Appeals are decided by panels of three judges sitting together on that case. The appellant presents legal arguments to the panel in a formal writing known as a «brief.» In the brief, the appellant tries to persuade the judges that the trial court made an error of law that warrants reversal. The party defending the appeal, the «appellee,» has the opportunity to file a responsive brief, in which the appellee tries to show why the trial court decision was correct, or why any error made by the trial court was not significant enough to have affected the outcome of the case and thus does not warrant reversal.

Some cases are decided on the basis of the parties' briefs. In other cases, the court orders that the parties appear for oral argument. Oral argument before the court of appeals is a structured discussion between the lawyers and the judges, which focuses on the legal issues in dispute. Each side is given a short time, usually about 15 minutes, to present its argument to the court. Members of the panel frequently intervene with questions to the lawyers.

The court will state the reasons for its decision, almost always in a written opinion which will set forth the facts and procedural history of the case, the issue, the court's holding, and the reasons for the court's decision. A judge on the panel who disagrees with the outcome of the majority decision may write a separate *dissenting* opinion. In some cases, a judge who agrees with the result reached but for a different or additional reason than that stated in the majority opinion may file a *concurring* opinion.

The court of appeals either *affirms* or *reverses* the lower court or agency decision. A reversal is often accompanied by a remand to the lower court or agency for additional proceedings. In the federal system, as discussed in Chapter II, rulings by one court of appeals bind the circuit, including the court of appeals itself.

The unsuccessful party before the court of appeals may seek additional review through a number of mechanisms, but such review is discretionary and infrequently granted. First, a losing party may seek *reconsideration* by the three-judge panel that ruled against that party. For reasons that should seem somewhat obvious, these requests are generally not successful. Second, a losing party may seek rehearing *en banc*. *En banc* review means that a larger number of judges beyond the original three-judge panel reviews the panel's decision. In almost every circuit, the *en banc* court will include all judges on that particular court of appeals. *En banc* review is rarely granted.

Finally, a losing party may also seek review by the United States Supreme Court. The Supreme Court's docket is largely discretionary, and the Court (as it is referred to) does not have to grant review except in a small number of cases governed by special statutes. In the vast majority of cases, Supreme Court review is discretionary under the Court's *certiorari* review. In any given

year, the United States Supreme Court will typically receive about 8,000 petitions for the writ of *certiorari*, and will agree to hear fewer than 100 of them.

The Supreme Court decides petitions for the writ of *certiorari* under the
so-called «Rule of Four.» If four of the nine justices vote in favor of granting
the writ of *certiorari*, then the writ will be granted and the case will be scheduled for briefing and, usually, oral argument. The Supreme Court typically will
agree to hear a case only when it involves an unusually important legal principle or when two or more federal courts or state courts of last resort have
interpreted a federal law differently. When the Supreme Court does hear a
case, the parties are required to file written briefs and the Court may order
oral argument. Other parties with significant interests in the legal issues raised
by a case may ask permission to file briefs as *amicus curiae* or «friends of the
court.» The executive branch, acting through the Solicitor General, will often
file such briefs.

If the Supreme Court refuses to grant the petition for *certiorari*, the Court
does not provide any explanation for its denial of the writ, although occasionally one or more of the justices will issue a dissent to the Court's order
declining to review the case. This is a statement of why he or she thinks that
the Court should have reviewed the case on its merits. The denial of the writ
of *certiorari* is not a decision on the merits of the case, and the Court has
cautioned that the denial of the writ is not to be interpreted as the Court's
endorsement or approval of the underlying decision.

There are nine members of the Supreme Court – the Chief Justice of the
United States and eight associate justices. They sit together *en banc*. As with
the court of appeals, the Court will only consider legal arguments and will
not consider new evidence.

The Supreme Court explains the reasons for its decision in a written opinion. Supreme Court decisions on questions of federal law are precedent for
all other courts in the United States. As with the courts of appeals, justices
may write dissenting or concurring opinions, a practice that has become very
common in recent years.

CONSTITUTION OF THE UNITED STATES OF AMERICA

[Preamble]

We the People of the United States, in Order to form a more perfect Union, establish Justice, insure domestic Tranquillity, provide for the common defence, promote the general Welfare, and secure the Blessings of Liberty to ourselves and our Posterity, do ordain and establish this Constitution for the United States of America.

Article I

Section 1.

All legislative Powers herein granted shall be vested in a Congress of the United States, which shall consist of a Senate and House of Representatives.

Section 2.

The House of Representatives shall be composed of Members chosen every second Year by the People of the several States, and the Electors in each State shall have the Qualifications requisite for Electors of the most numerous Branch of the State Legislature.

No Person shall be a Representative who shall not have attained to the age of twenty five Years, and been seven Years a Citizen of the United States, and who shall not, when elected, be an Inhabitant of that State in which he shall be chosen.

Representatives and direct Taxes shall be apportioned among the several States which may be included within this Union, according to their respective Numbers, which shall be determined by adding to the whole Number of free Persons, including those bound to Service for a Term of Years, and excluding Indians not taxed, three fifths of all other Persons. The actual Enumeration shall be made within three Years after the first Meeting of the Congress of the United States, and within every subsequent Term of ten Years, in such Manner as they shall by Law direct. The Number of Representatives shall not exceed one for every thirty Thousand, but each State shall have at Least one Representative; and until such enumeration shall be made, the State of New Hampshire shall be entitled to chuse three, Massachusetts eight, Rhode-Island and Providence Plantations one, Connecticut five, New-York six, New Jersey four,

Pennsylvania eight, Delaware one, Maryland six, Virginia ten, North Carolina five, South Carolina five, and Georgia three.

When vacancies happen in the Representation from any State, the Executive Authority thereof shall issue Writs of Election to fill such Vacancies.

The House of Representatives shall chuse their Speaker and other Officers; and shall have the sole Power of Impeachment.

Section 3.

The Senate of the United States shall be composed of two Senators from each State, chosen by the Legislature thereof, for six Years; and each Senator shall have one Vote.

Immediately after they shall be assembled in Consequence of the first Election, they shall be divided as equally as may be into three Classes. The Seats of the Senators of the first Class shall be vacated at the Expiration of the second Year, of the second Class at the Expiration of the fourth Year, and of the third Class at the Expiration of the sixth Year, so that one third may be chosen every second Year; and if Vacancies happen by Resignation, or otherwise, during the Recess of the Legislature of any State, the Executive thereof may make temporary Appointments until the next Meeting of the Legislature, which shall then fill such Vacancies.

No Person shall be a Senator who shall not have attained to the Age of thirty Years, and been nine Years a Citizen of the United States, and who shall not, when elected, be an Inhabitant of that State for which he shall be chosen.

The Vice President of the United States shall be President of the Senate but shall have no Vote, unless they be equally divided.

The Senate shall chuse their other Officers, and also a President pro tempore, in the Absence of the Vice President, or when he shall exercise the Office of President of the United States.

The Senate shall have the sole Power to try all Impeachments. When sitting for that Purpose, they shall be on Oath or Affirmation. When the President of the United States is tried the Chief Justice shall preside: And no Person shall be convicted without the Concurrence of two thirds of the Members present.

Judgment in Cases of Impeachment shall not extend further than to removal from Office, and disqualification to hold and enjoy any Office of honor, Trust or Profit under the United States: but the Party convicted shall nevertheless be liable and subject to Indictment, Trial, Judgment and Punishment, according to Law.

Section 4.

The Times, Places and Manner of holding Elections for Senators and Representatives, shall be prescribed in each State by the Legislature thereof; but the Congress may at any time by Law make or alter such Regulations, except as to the Places of chusing Senators.

The Congress shall assemble at least once in every Year, and such Meeting shall be on the first Monday in December, unless they shall by Law appoint a different Day.

Section 5.

Each House shall be the Judge of the Elections, Returns and Qualifications of its own Members, and a Majority of each shall constitute a Quorum to do Business; but a smaller Number may adjourn from day to day, and may be authorized to compel the Attendance of absent Members, in such Manner, and under such Penalties as each House may provide.

Each House may determine the Rules of its Proceedings, punish its Members for disorderly Behaviour, and, with the Concurrence of two thirds, expel a Member.

Each House shall keep a Journal of its Proceedings, and from time to time publish the same, excepting such Parts as may in their Judgment require Secrecy; and the Yeas and Nays of the Members of either House on any question shall, at the Desire of one fifth of those Present, be entered on the Journal.

Neither House, during the Session of Congress, shall, without the Consent of the other, adjourn for more than three days, nor to any other Place than that in which the two Houses shall be sitting.

Section 6.

The Senators and Representatives shall receive a Compensation for their Services, to be ascertained by Law, and paid out of the Treasury of the United States. They shall in all Cases, except Treason, Felony and Breach of the Peace, be privileged from Arrest during their Attendance at the Session of their respective Houses, and in going to and returning from the same; and for any Speech or Debate in either House, they shall not be questioned in any other Place.

No Senator or Representative shall, during the Time for which he was elected, be appointed to any civil Office under the Authority of the United States, which shall have been created, or the Emoluments whereof shall have been encreased during such time; and no Person holding any Office under the United States, shall be a Member of either House during his Continuance in Office.

Section 7.

All Bills for raising Revenue shall originate in the House of Representatives; but the Senate may propose or concur with amendments as on other Bills.

Every Bill which shall have passed the House of Representatives and the Senate, shall, before it become a law, be presented to the President of the

United States: If he approve he shall sign it, but if not he shall return it, with his Objections to that House in which it shall have originated, who shall enter the Objections at large on their Journal, and proceed to reconsider it. If after such Reconsideration two thirds of that House shall agree to pass the Bill, it shall be sent, together with the Objections, to the other House, by which it shall likewise be reconsidered, and if approved by two thirds of that House, it shall become a Law. But in all such Cases the Votes of both Houses shall be determined by Yeas and Nays, and the Names of the Persons voting for and against the Bill shall be entered on the Journal of each House respectively. If any Bill shall not be returned by the President within ten Days (Sundays excepted) after it shall have been presented to him, the Same shall be a Law, in like Manner as if he had signed it, unless the Congress by their Adjournment prevent its Return, in which Case it shall not be a Law

Every Order, Resolution, or Vote to which the Concurrence of the Senate and House of Representatives may be necessary (except on a question of Adjournment) shall be presented to the President of the United States; and before the Same shall take Effect, shall be approved by him, or being disapproved by him, shall be repassed by two thirds of the Senate and House of Representatives, according to the Rules and Limitations prescribed in the Case of a Bill.

Section 8.

The Congress shall have Power To lay and collect Taxes, Duties, Imposts and Excises, to pay the Debts and provide for the common Defence and general Welfare of the United States; but all Duties, Imposts and Excises shall be uniform throughout the United States;

To borrow Money on the credit of the United States;

To regulate Commerce with foreign Nations, and among the several States, and with the Indian Tribes;

To establish an uniform Rule of Naturalization, and uniform Laws on the subject of Bankruptcies throughout the United States;

To coin Money, regulate the Value thereof, and of foreign Coin, and fix the Standard of Weights and Measures;

To provide for the Punishment of counterfeiting the Securities and current Coin of the United States;

To establish Post Offices and post Roads;

To promote the Progress of Science and useful Arts, by securing for limited Times to Authors and Inventors the exclusive Right to their respective Writings and Discoveries;

To constitute Tribunals inferior to the supreme Court;

To define and punish Piracies and Felonies committed on the high Seas, and Offences against the Law of Nations;

To declare War, grant Letters of Marque and Reprisal, and make Rules concerning Captures on Land and Water;

To raise and support Armies, but no Appropriation of Money to that Use shall be for a longer Term than two Years;

To provide and maintain a Navy;

To make Rules for the Government and Regulation of the land and naval Forces;

To provide for calling forth the Militia to execute the Laws of the Union, suppress Insurrections and repeal Invasions;

To provide for organizing, arming, and disciplining, the Militia, and for governing such Part of them as may be employed in the Service of the United States, reserving to the States respectively, the Appointment of the Officers, and the Authority of training the Militia according to the discipline prescribed by Congress;

To exercise exclusive Legislation in all Cases whatsoever, over such District (not exceeding ten Miles square) as may, by Cession of Particular States, and the Acceptance of Congress, become the Seat of the Government of the United States, and to exercise like Authority over all Places purchased by the Consent of the Legislature of the State in which the Same shall be, for the Erection of Forts, Magazines, Arsenals, dock-Yards and other needful Buildings;--And To make all Laws which shall be necessary and proper for carrying into Execution the foregoing Powers and all other Powers vested by this Constitution in the Government of the United States, or in any Department or Officer thereof.

Section 9.

The Migration or Importation of such Persons as any of the States now existing shall think proper to admit, shall not be prohibited by the Congress prior to the Year one thousand eight hundred and eight, but a Tax or duty may be imposed on such Importation, not exceeding ten dollars for each Person.

The Privilege of the Writ of Habeas Corpus shall not be suspended, unless when in Cases or Rebellion or Invasion the public Safety may require it.

No Bill of Attainder or ex post facto Law shall be passed.

No Capitation, or other direct, Tax shall be laid, unless in Proportion to the Census of Enumeration herein before directed to be taken.

No Tax or Duty shall be laid on Articles exported from any State.

No Preference shall be given by any Regulation of Commerce or Revenue to the Ports of one State over those of another: nor shall Vessels bound to, or from, one State, be obliged to enter, clear or pay Duties in another.

No Money shall be drawn from the Treasury, but in Consequence of Appropriations made by Law; and a regular Statement and Account of the Receipts and Expenditures of all public Money shall be published from time to time.

No Title of Nobility shall be granted by the United States: And no Person holding any Office of Profit or Trust under them, shall, without the Consent of the Congress, accept of any present, Emolument, Office, or Title, of any kind whatever, from any King, Prince or foreign State.

Section 10.

No State shall enter into any Treaty, Alliance, or Confederation; grant Letters of Marque and Reprisal; coin Money; emit Bills of Credit; make any Thing but gold and silver Coin a Tender in Payment of Debts; pass any Bill of Attainder, ex post facto Law, or Law impairing the Obligation of Contracts, or grant any Title of Nobility.

No State shall, without the Consent of the Congress, lay any Imposts or Duties on Imports or Exports, except what may be absolutely necessary for executing it's inspection Laws: and the net Produce of all Duties and Imposts, laid by any State on Imports or Exports, shall be for the Use of the Treasury of the United States; and all such Laws shall be subject to the Revision and Controul of the Congress.

No State shall, without the Consent of Congress, lay any Duty of Tonnage, keep Troops, or Ships of War in time of Peace, enter into any Agreement or Compact with another State, or with a foreign Power, or engage in War, unless actually invaded, or in such imminent Danger as will not admit of delay.

Article II

Section 1.

The executive Power shall be vested in a President of the United States of America. He shall hold his Office during the Term of four Years, and, together with the Vice President, chosen for the same Term, be elected, as follows:

Each State shall appoint, in such Manner as the Legislature thereof may direct, a Number of Electors, equal to the whole Number of Senators and Representatives to which the State may be entitled in the Congress: but no Senator or Representative, or Person holding an Office of Trust or Profit under the United States, shall be appointed an Elector.

The Electors shall meet in their respective States, and vote by Ballot for two Persons, of whom one at least shall not be an Inhabitant of the same State with themselves. And they shall make a List of all the Persons voted for, and of the Number of Votes for each; which List they shall sign and certify, and transmit sealed to the Seat of the Government of the United States, directed to the President of the Senate. The President of the Senate shall, in the Presence of the Senate and House of Representatives, open all the Certificates, and the Votes shall then be counted. The Person having the greatest Number of Votes shall be the President, if such Number be a Majority of the whole Number of Electors appointed; and if there be more than one who have such Majority, and have an equal Number of Votes, then the House of Representatives shall immediately chuse by Ballot one of them for President; and if no Person have a Majority, then from the five highest on the List the said House shall in like Manner chuse the President. But in chusing the President, the Votes shall be taken by States, the Representatives from each State having one Vote; a quorum for this Purpose shall consist of a Member or Members from two thirds of the States, and a Majority of all the States shall be necessary to a Choice. In every Case, after the Choice of the President, the Person having the greatest Number of Votes of the Electors shall be the Vice President. But if there should remain two or more who have equal Votes, the Senate shall chuse from them by Ballot the Vice President.

The Congress may determine the Time of chusing the Electors, and the Day on which they shall give their Votes; which Day shall be the same throughout the United States.

No Person except a natural born Citizen, or a Citizen of the United States, at the time of the Adoption of this Constitution, shall be eligible to the Office of President; neither shall any person be eligible to that Office who shall not have attained to the Age of thirty five Years, and been fourteen Years a Resident within the United States.

In Case of the Removal of the President from Office, or of his Death, Resignation, or Inability to discharge the Powers and Duties of the said Office, the Same shall devolve on the Vice President, and the Congress may by Law provide for the Case of Removal, Death, Resignation or Inability, both of the President and Vice President, declaring what Officer shall then act as President, and such Officer shall act accordingly, until the Disability be removed, or a President shall be elected.

The President shall, at stated Times, receive for his Services, a Compensation, which shall neither be encreased nor diminished during the Period for which he shall have been elected, and he shall not receive within that Period any other Emolument from the United States, or any of them.

Before he enter on the Execution of his Office, he shall take the following Oath or Affirmation: «I do solemnly swear (or affirm) that I will faithfully execute the Office of President of the United States, and will to the best of my Ability, preserve, protect and defend the Constitution of the United States».

Section 2.

The President shall be Commander in Chief of the Army and Navy of the United States, and of the Militia of the several States, when called into the actual Service of the United States; he may require the Opinion, in writing, of the principal Officer in each of the executive Departments, upon any Subject relating to the Duties of their respective Offices, and he shall have Power to Grant Reprieves and Pardons for Offences against the United States, except in Cases of Impeachment.

He shall have Power, by and with the Advice and Consent of the Senate, to make Treaties, provided two thirds of the Senators present concur; and he shall nominate, and by and with the Advice and Consent of the Senate, shall appoint Ambassadors, other public Ministers and Consuls, Judges of the supreme Court, and all other Officers of the United States, whose Appointments are not herein otherwise provided for, and which shall be established by Law: but the Congress may by Law vest the Appointment of such inferior Officers, as they think proper, in the President alone, in the Courts of Law, or in the Heads of Departments.

The President shall have Power to fill up all Vacancies that may happen during the Recess of the Senate, by granting Commissions which shall expire at the End of their next Session.

Section 3.

He shall from time to time give to the Congress Information on the State of the Union, and recommend to their Consideration such Measures as he shall judge necessary and expedient; he may, on extraordinary Occasions, convene both Houses, or either of them, and in Case of Disagreement between them, with Respect to the Time of Adjournment, he may adjourn them to such Time as he shall think proper; he shall receive Ambassadors and other public Ministers; he shall take Care that the Laws be faithfully executed, and shall Commission all the Officers of the United States.

Section 4.

The President, Vice President and all Civil Officers of the United States, shall be removed from Office on Impeachment for and Conviction of, Treason, Bribery, or other high Crimes and Misdemeanors.

Article III

Section 1.

The judicial Power of the United States, shall be vested in one supreme Court, and in such inferior Courts as the Congress may from time to time ordain and establish. The Judges, both of the supreme and inferior Courts, shall hold their Offices during good Behaviour, and shall, at stated Times, receive for their Services, a Compensation, which shall not be diminished during their Continuance in Office.

Section 2.

The judicial Power shall extend to all Cases, in Law and Equity, arising under this Constitution, the Laws of the United States, and Treaties made, or which shall be made, under their Authority;--to all Cases affecting Ambassadors, other public ministers and Consuls;--to all Cases of admiralty and maritime Jurisdiction;--to Controversies to which the United States shall be a Party;--to Controversies between two or more States;--between a State and Citizens of another State;--between Citizens of different States;--between Citizens of the same State claiming Lands under Grants of different States, and between a State, or the Citizens thereof, and foreign States, Citizens or Subjects.

In all Cases affecting Ambassadors, other public Ministers and Consuls, and those in which a State shall be Party, the supreme Court shall have original Jurisdiction. In all the other Cases before mentioned, the supreme Court shall have appellate Jurisdiction, both as to Law and Fact, with such Exceptions, and under such Regulations as the Congress shall make.

The Trial of all Crimes, except in Cases of Impeachment, shall be by Jury; and such Trial shall be held in the State where the said Crimes shall have been committed; but when not committed within any State, the Trial shall be at such Place or Places as the Congress may by Law have directed.

Section 3.

Treason against the United States, shall consist only in levying War against them, or in adhering to their Enemies, giving them Aid and Comfort. No Person shall be convicted of Treason unless on the Testimony of two Witnesses to the same overt Act, or on Confession in open Court.

The Congress shall have Power to declare the Punishment of Treason, but no Attainder of Treason shall work Corruption of Blood, or Forfeiture except during the Life of the Person attainted.

Article IV

Section 1.

Full Faith and Credit shall be given in each State to the public Acts, Records, and judicial Proceedings of every other State. And the Congress may by general Laws prescribe the Manner in which such Acts, Records and Proceedings shall be proved, and the Effect thereof.

Section 2.

The Citizens of each State shall be entitled to all Privileges and Immunities of Citizens in the several States.

A Person charged in any State with Treason, Felony, or other Crime, who shall flee from Justice, and be found in another State, shall on Demand of the executive Authority of the State from which he fled, be delivered up, to be removed to the State having Jurisdiction of the Crime.

No Person held to Service or Labour in one State, under the Laws thereof, escaping into another, shall, in Consequence of any Law or Regulation therein, be discharged from such Service or Labour, but shall be delivered up on Claim of the Party to whom such Service or Labour may be due.

Section 3.

New States may be admitted by the Congress into this Union; but no new State shall be formed or erected within the Jurisdiction of any other State; nor any State be formed by the Junction of two or more States, or Parts of States, without the Consent of the Legislatures of the States concerned as well as of the Congress.

The Congress shall have Power to dispose of and make all needful Rules and Regulations respecting the Territory or other Property belonging to the United States; and nothing in this Constitution shall be so construed as to Prejudice any Claims of the United States, or of any particular State.

Section 4.

The United States shall guarantee to every State in this Union a Republican Form of Government, and shall protect each of them against Invasion; and on Application of the Legislature, or of the Executive (when the Legislature cannot be convened) against domestic Violence.

Article V

The Congress, whenever two thirds of both Houses shall deem it necessary, shall propose Amendments to this Constitution, or, on the Application of the Legislatures of two thirds of the several States, shall call a Convention for proposing Amendments, which, in either Case, shall be valid to all Intents and Purposes, as Part of this Constitution, when ratified by the Legislatures of three fourths of the several States, or by Conventions in three fourths thereof, as the one or the other Mode of Ratification may be proposed by the Congress; Provided that no Amendment which may be made prior to the Year One thousand eight hundred and eight shall in any Manner affect the first and fourth Clauses in the Ninth Section of the first Article; and that no State, without its Consent, shall be deprived of its equal Suffrage in the Senate.

Article VI

All Debts contracted and Engagements entered into, before the Adoption of this Constitution, shall be as valid against the United States under this Constitution, as under the Confederation.

This Constitution, and the Laws of the United States which shall be made in Pursuance thereof; and all Treaties made, or which shall be made, under the Authority of the United States, shall be the supreme Law of the Land; and the Judges in every State shall be bound thereby, any Thing in the Constitution or Laws of any state to the Contrary notwithstanding.

The Senators and Representatives before mentioned, and the Members of the several State Legislatures, and all executive and judicial Officers, both of the United States and of the several States, shall be bound by Oath or Affirmation, to support this Constitution; but no religious Test shall ever be required as a Qualification to any Office or public Trust under the United States.

Article VII

The Ratification of the Conventions of nine States, shall be sufficient for the Establishment of this Constitution between the States so ratifying the same.

Amendments to the Constitution of the United States of America

Amendment I

Congress shall make no law respecting an establishment of religion, or prohibiting the free exercise thereof; or abridging the freedom of speech, or of the press; or the right of the people peaceably to assemble, and to petition the Government for a redress of grievances.

Amendment II

A well regulated Militia, being necessary to the security of a free State, the right of the people to keep and bear Arms, shall not be infringed.

Amendment III

No Soldier shall, in time of peace be quartered in any house, without the consent of the Owner, nor in time of war, but in a manner to be prescribed by law.

Amendment IV

The right of the people to be secure in their persons, houses, papers, and effects, against unreasonable searches and seizures, shall not be violated, and no Warrants shall issue, but upon probable cause, supported by Oath or affirmation, and particularly describing the place to be searched, and the persons or things to be seized.

Amendment V

No person shall be held to answer for a capital, or otherwise infamous crime, unless on a presentment or indictment of a Grand Jury, except in cases arising in the land or naval forces, or in the Militia, when in actual service in time of War or public danger; nor shall any person be subject for the same offence to be twice put in jeopardy of life or limb; nor shall be compelled in any criminal case to be a witness against himself, nor be deprived of life, liberty, or property, without due process of law; nor shall private property be taken for public use, without just compensation.

Amendment VI

In all criminal prosecutions, the accused shall enjoy the right to a speedy and public trial, by an impartial jury of the State and district wherein the crime shall have been committed, which district shall have been previously ascertained by law, and to be informed of the nature and cause of the accusation; to be confronted with the witnesses against him; to have compulsory process for obtaining witnesses in his favor, and to have the Assistance of Counsel for his defence.

Amendment VII

In Suits at common law, where the value in controversy shall exceed twenty dollars, the right of trial by jury shall be preserved, and no fact tried by a jury, shall be otherwise re-examined in any Court of the United States, than according to the rules of the common law.

Amendment VIII

Excessive bail shall not be required, nor excessive fines imposed, nor cruel and unusual punishments inflicted.

Amendment IX

The enumeration in the Constitution, of certain rights, shall not be construed to deny or disparage others retained by the people.

Amendment X

The powers not delegated to the United States by the Constitution, nor prohibited by it to the States, are reserved to the States respectively, or to the people.

Amendment XI

The Judicial power of the United States shall not be construed to extend to any suit in law or equity, commenced or prosecuted against one of the United States by Citizens of another State, or by Citizens or Subjects of any Foreign State.

Amendment XII

The Electors shall meet in their respective states and vote by ballot for President and Vice-President, one of whom, at least, shall not be an inhabitant of the same state with themselves; they shall name in their ballots the person voted for as President, and in distinct ballots the person voted for as Vice–President, and they shall make distinct lists of all persons voted for as President, and of all persons voted for as Vice-President, and of the number of votes for each, which lists they shall sign and certify, and transmit sealed to the seat of the government of the United States, directed to the President of the Senate;--The President of the Senate shall, in the presence of the Senate and House of Representatives, open all the certificates and the votes shall then be counted;--The person having the greatest Number of votes for President, shall be the President, if such number be a majority of the whole number of Electors appointed; and if no person have such majority, then from the persons having the highest numbers not exceeding three on the list of those voted for as President, the House of Representatives shall choose immediately, by ballot, the President. But in choosing the President, the votes shall be taken by states, the representation from each state having one vote; a quorum for this purpose shall consist of a member or members from two-thirds of the states, and a majority of all the states shall be necessary to a choice. And if the House of Representatives shall not choose a President whenever the right of choice shall devolve upon them, before the fourth day of March next following, then the Vice– President shall act as President, as in the case of the death or other constitutional disability of the President--The person having the greatest number of votes as Vice-President, shall be the Vice-President, if such number be a majority of the whole number of Electors appointed, and if no person have a majority, then from the two highest numbers on the list, the Senate shall choose the Vice-President; a quorum for the purpose shall consist of two-thirds of the whole number of Senators, and a majority of the whole number shall be necessary to a choice. But no person constitutionally ineligible to the office of President shall be eligible to that of Vice-President of the United States.

Amendment XIII

Section 1. Neither slavery nor involuntary servitude, except as a punishment for crime whereof the party shall have been duly convicted, shall exist within the United States, or any place subject to their jurisdiction.

Section 2. Congress shall have power to enforce this article by appropriate legislation.

Amendment XIV

Section. 1. All persons born or naturalized in the United States and subject to the jurisdiction thereof, are citizens of the United States and of the State wherein they reside. No State shall make or enforce any law which shall abridge the privileges or immunities of citizens of the United States; nor shall any State deprive any person of life, liberty, or property, without due process of law; nor deny to any person within its jurisdiction the equal protection of the laws.

Section. 2. Representatives shall be apportioned among the several States according to their respective numbers, counting the whole number of persons in each State, excluding Indians not taxed. But when the right to vote at any election for the choice of electors for President and Vice President of the United States, Representatives in Congress, the Executive and Judicial officers of a State, or the members of the Legislature thereof, is denied to any of the male inhabitants of such State, being twenty-one years of age, and citizens of the United States, or in any way abridged, except for participation in rebellion, or other crime, the basis of representation therein shall be reduced in the proportion which the number of such male citizens shall bear to the whole number of male citizens twenty-one years of age in such State.

Section. 3. No person shall be a Senator or Representative in Congress, or elector of President and Vice President, or hold any office, civil or military, under the United States, or under any State, who, having previously taken an oath, as a member of Congress, or as an officer of the United States, or as a member of any State legislature, or as an executive or judicial officer of any State, to support the Constitution of the United States, shall have engaged in insurrection or rebellion against the same, or given aid or comfort to the enemies thereof. But Congress may by a vote of two-thirds of each House, remove such disability.

Section. 4. The validity of the public debt of the United States, authorized by law, including debts incurred for payment of pensions and bounties for services in suppressing insurrection or rebellion, shall not be questioned. But neither the United States nor any State shall assume or pay any debt or obligation incurred in aid of insurrection or rebellion against the United States, or any claim for the loss or emancipation of any slave; but all such debts, obligations and claims shall be held illegal and void.

Section. 5. The Congress shall have power to enforce, by appropriate legislation, the provisions of this article.

Amendment XV

Section. 1. The right of citizens of the United States to vote shall not be denied or abridged by the United States or by any State on account of race, color, or previous condition of servitude.

Section. 2. The Congress shall have power to enforce this article by appropriate legislation.

Amendment XVI

The Congress shall have power to lay and collect taxes on incomes, from whatever source derived, without apportionment among the several States, and without regard to any census or enumeration.

Amendment XVII

The Senate of the United States shall be composed of two Senators from each State, elected by the people thereof, for six years; and each Senator shall have one vote. The electors in each State shall have the qualifications requisite for electors of the most numerous branch of the State legislatures.

When vacancies happen in the representation of any State in the Senate, the executive authority of such State shall issue writs of election to fill such vacancies: Provided, That the legislature of any State may empower the executive thereof to make temporary appointments until the people fill the vacancies by election as the legislature may direct.

This amendment shall not be so construed as to affect the election or term of any Senator chosen before it becomes valid as part of the Constitution.

Amendment XVIII

Section. 1. After one year from the ratification of this article the manufacture, sale, or transportation of intoxicating liquors within, the importation thereof into, or the exportation thereof from the United States and all territory subject to the jurisdiction thereof for beverage purposes is hereby prohibited.

Sec. 2. The Congress and the several States shall have concurrent power to enforce this article by appropriate legislation.

Sec. 3. This article shall be inoperative unless it shall have been ratified as an amendment to the Constitution by the legislatures of the several States, as provided in the Constitution, within seven years from the date of the submission hereof to the States by the Congress.

Amendment XIX

The right of citizens of the United States to vote shall not be denied or abridged by the United States or by any State on account of sex. Congress shall have power to enforce this article by appropriate legislation.

Amendment XX

Section. 1. The terms of the President and Vice President shall end at noon on the 20th day of January, and the terms of Senators and Representatives at noon on the 3d day of January, of the years in which such terms would have ended if this article had not been ratified; and the terms of their successors shall then begin.

Sec. 2. The Congress shall assemble at least once in every year, and such meeting shall begin at noon on the 3d day of January, unless they shall by law appoint a different day.

Sec. 3. If, at the time fixed for the beginning of the term of the President, the President elect shall have died, the Vice President elect shall become President. If a President shall not have been chosen before the time fixed for the beginning of his term, or if the President elect shall have failed to qualify, then the Vice President elect shall act as President until a President shall have qualified; and the Congress may by law provide for the case wherein neither a President elect nor a Vice President elect shall have qualified, declaring who shall then act as President, or the manner in which one who is to act shall be selected, and such person shall act accordingly until a President or Vice President shall have qualified.

Sec. 4. The Congress may by law provide for the case of the death of any of the persons from whom the House of Representatives may choose a President whenever the right of choice shall have devolved upon them, and for the case of the death of any of the persons from whom the Senate may choose a Vice President whenever the right of choice shall have devolved upon them.

Sec. 5. Sections 1 and 2 shall take effect on the 15th day of October following the ratification of this article.

Sec. 6. This article shall be inoperative unless it shall have been ratified as an amendment to the Constitution by the legislatures of three-fourths of the several States within seven years from the date of its submission.

Amendment XXI

Section. 1. The eighteenth article of amendment to the Constitution of the United States is hereby repealed.

Sec. 2. The transportation or importation into any State, Territory, or possession of the United States for delivery or use therein of intoxicating liquors, in violation of the laws thereof, is hereby prohibited.

Sec. 3. This article shall be inoperative unless it shall have been ratified as an amendment to the Constitution by conventions in the several States, as provided in the Constitution, within seven years from the date of the submission hereof to the States by the Congress.

Amendment XXII

Section. 1. No person shall be elected to the office of the President more than twice, and no person who has held the office of President, or acted as President, for more than two years of a term to which some other person was elected President shall be elected to the office of the President more than once. But this Article shall not apply to any person holding the office of President, when this Article was proposed by the Congress, and shall not prevent any person who may be holding the office of President, or acting as President, during the term within which this Article becomes operative from holding the office of President or acting as President during the remainder of such term.

Sec. 2. This article shall be inoperative unless it shall have been ratified as an amendment to the Constitution by the legislatures of three-fourths of the several States within seven years from the date of its submission to the States by the Congress.

Amendment XXIII

Section. 1. The District constituting the seat of Government of the United States shall appoint in such manner as the Congress may direct: A number of electors of President and Vice President equal to the whole number of Senators and Representatives in Congress to which the District would be entitled if it were a State, but in no event more than the least populous State; they shall be in addition to those appointed by the States, but they shall be considered, for the purposes of the election of President and Vice President, to be electors appointed by a State; and they shall meet in the District and perform such duties as provided by the twelfth article of amendment.

Sec. 2. The Congress shall have power to enforce this article by appropriate legislation.

Amendment XXIV

Section. 1. The right of citizens of the United States to vote in any primary or other election for President or Vice President, for electors for President or Vice President, or for Senator or Representative in Congress, shall not be denied or abridged by the United States or any State by reason of failure to pay any poll tax or other tax.

Section. 2. The Congress shall have power to enforce this article by appropriate legislation.

Amendment XXV

Section. 1. In case of the removal of the President from office or of his death or resignation, the Vice President shall become President.

Section. 2. Whenever there is a vacancy in the office of the Vice President, the President shall nominate a Vice President who shall take office upon confirmation by a majority vote of both Houses of Congress.

Section. 3. Whenever the President transmits to the President pro tempore of the Senate and the Speaker of the House of Representatives has written declaration that he is unable to discharge the powers and duties of his office, and until he transmits to them a written declaration to the contrary, such powers and duties shall be discharged by the Vice President as Acting President.

Section. 4. Whenever the Vice President and a majority of either the principal officers of the executive departments or of such other body as Congress may by law provide, transmit to the President pro tempore of the Senate and the Speaker of the House of Representatives their written declaration that the President is unable to discharge the powers and duties of his office, the Vice

President shall immediately assume the powers and duties of the office as Acting President.

Thereafter, when the President transmits to the President pro tempore of the Senate and the Speaker of the House of Representatives has written declaration that no inability exists, he shall resume the powers and duties of his office unless the Vice President and a majority of either the principal officers of the executive department or of such other body as Congress may by law provide, transmit within four days to the President pro tempore of the Senate and the Speaker of the House of Representatives their written declaration that the President is unable to discharge the powers and duties of his office. Thereupon Congress shall decide the issue, assembling within forty-eight hours for that purpose if not in session. If the Congress, within twenty-one days after receipt of the latter written declaration, or, if Congress is not in session, within twenty-one days after Congress is required to assemble, determines by two-thirds vote of both Houses that the President is unable to discharge the powers and duties of his office, the Vice President shall continue to discharge the same as Acting President; otherwise, the President shall resume the powers and duties of his office.

Amendment XXVI

Section. 1. The right of citizens of the United States, who are eighteen years of age or older, to vote shall not be denied or abridged by the United States or by any State on account of age.

Section. 2. The Congress shall have power to enforce this article by appropriate legislation.

Amendment XXVII

No law varying the compensation for the services of the Senators and Representatives shall take effect, until an election of Representatives shall have intervened.

GEOGRAPHIC BOUNDARIES OF THE UNITED STATES COURTS OF APPEALS AND UNITED STATES DISTRICT COURTS

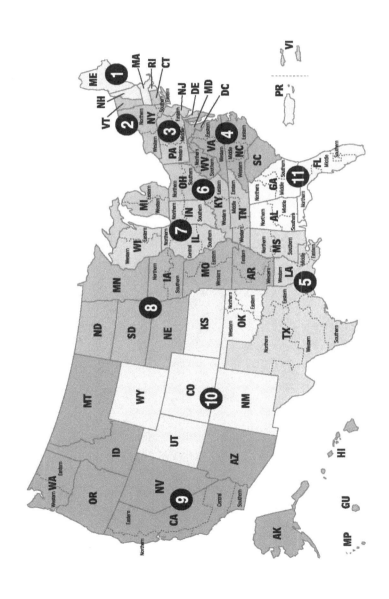

TEMPLATE OF AN INTEROFFICE MEMORANDUM

**PRIVILEGED AND CONFIDENTIAL ATTORNEY
WORK PRODUCT**

MEMORANDUM

TO: [Supervisor's full, formal name; no titles]
FROM: [Your full, formal name; no titles; initial final]
DATE: [Month day, year]
RE: [One phrase; include client, legal issue, a few material facts]

QUESTION[S] PRESENTED

[1.]*

[Questions Presented should essentially state the legal issue(s) addressed in the memo. The Questions Presented become in substance the major point headings for the Legal Discussion, infra.]

2.

BRIEF ANSWER[S]

[1.]*

[There will be a Brief Answer for each Question Presented.]

2.

STATEMENT OF FACTS

[No headings, formal sections, or numbered paragraphs. Use traditional paragraph format. Standard paragraph format in the U.S. requires one tab at the start of a paragraph with a double space between all lines, including before a new paragraph.]

   * If you do not have at least two entries at any particular level, there should be no alphabetical or numerical designations.

LEGAL DISCUSSION

[Use introductory text as may be appropriate.]

[I.]*   FIRST MAJOR POINT HEADING**

[Use introductory text as may be appropriate immediately after any point heading.]

A.   Divide Major Issue Into Subsidiary Issues.

    1.   Further divisions can be made.*

    2.   Break down your analysis as much as feasible.

B.   Taken Together, Headings should give the Reader a Summary of your Analysis.

C.   Make Sure that your Headings are Internally Consistent.

    1.   Sub-headings must relate to the major point heading that precedes them.

    2.   All headings at the same level should be presented in the same style.

II.   SECOND MAJOR POINT HEADING

[Use subheadings as above.]

CONCLUSION

[No headings, formal sections, or numbered paragraphs. Use traditional paragraph format.]

**Note that Roman numerals are followed by capital letters, which are followed by Arabic numerals, followed by lower case letters, etc.